Fantastic **Arya Bàhram**

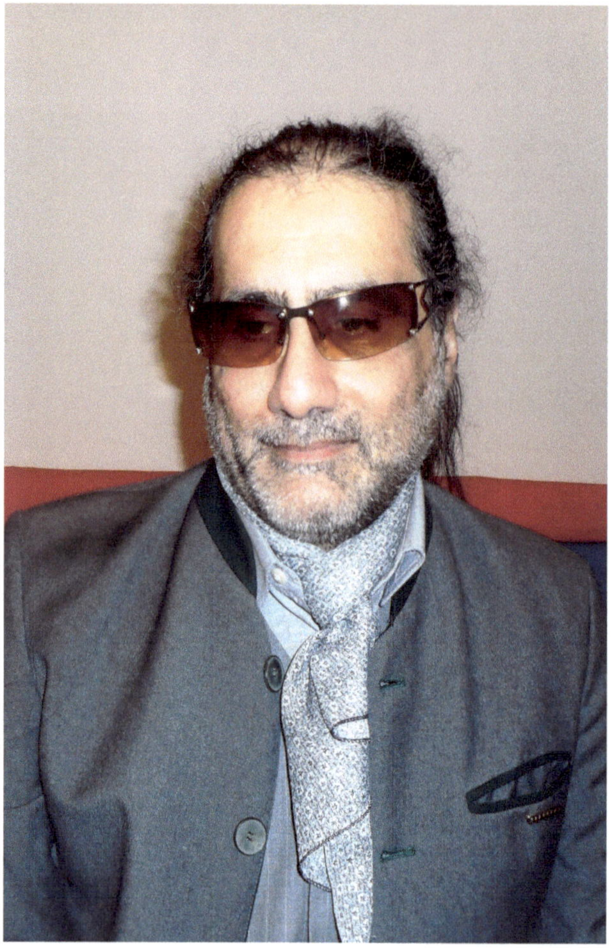

Fantastic Arya Bàhram

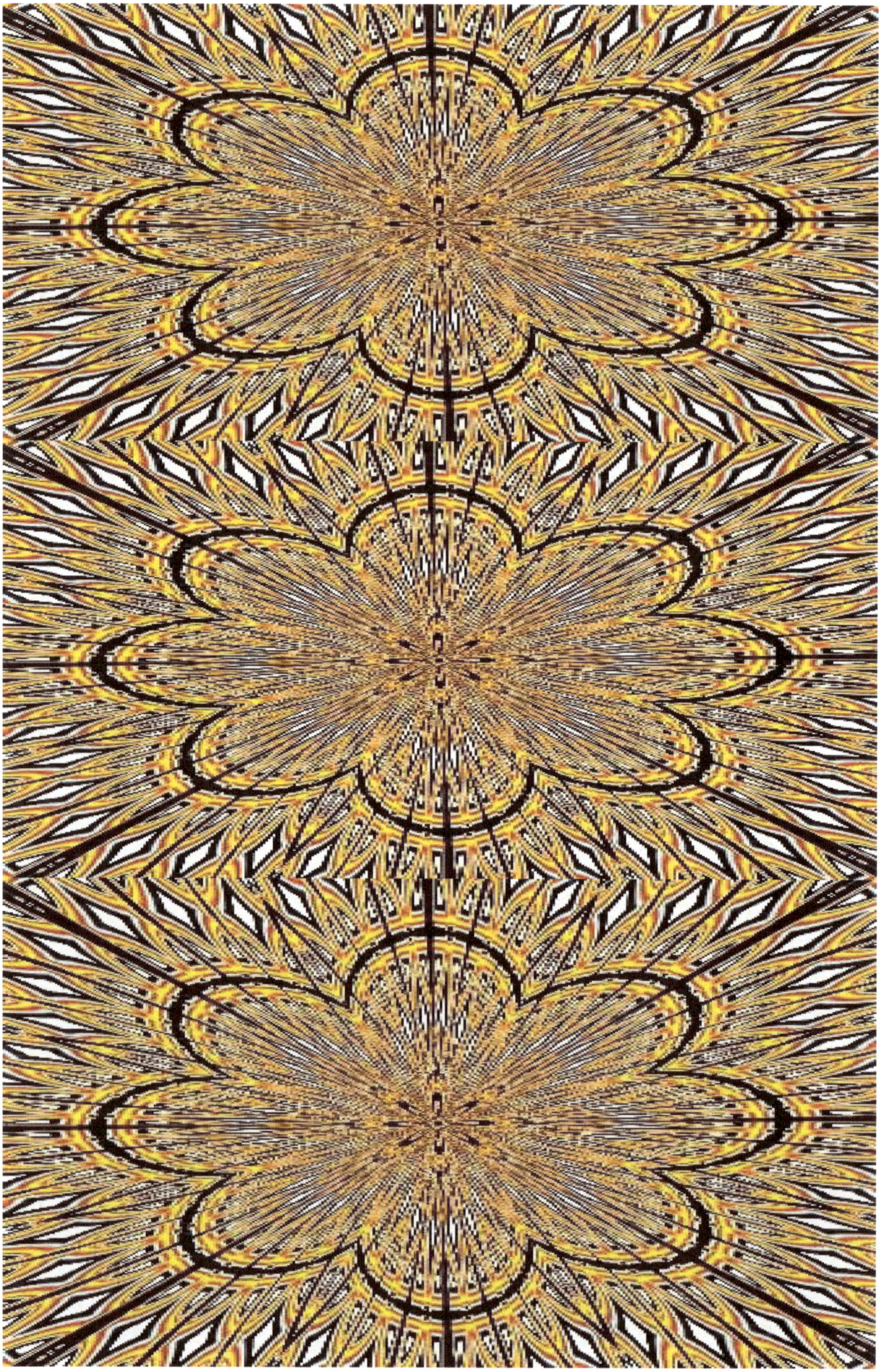

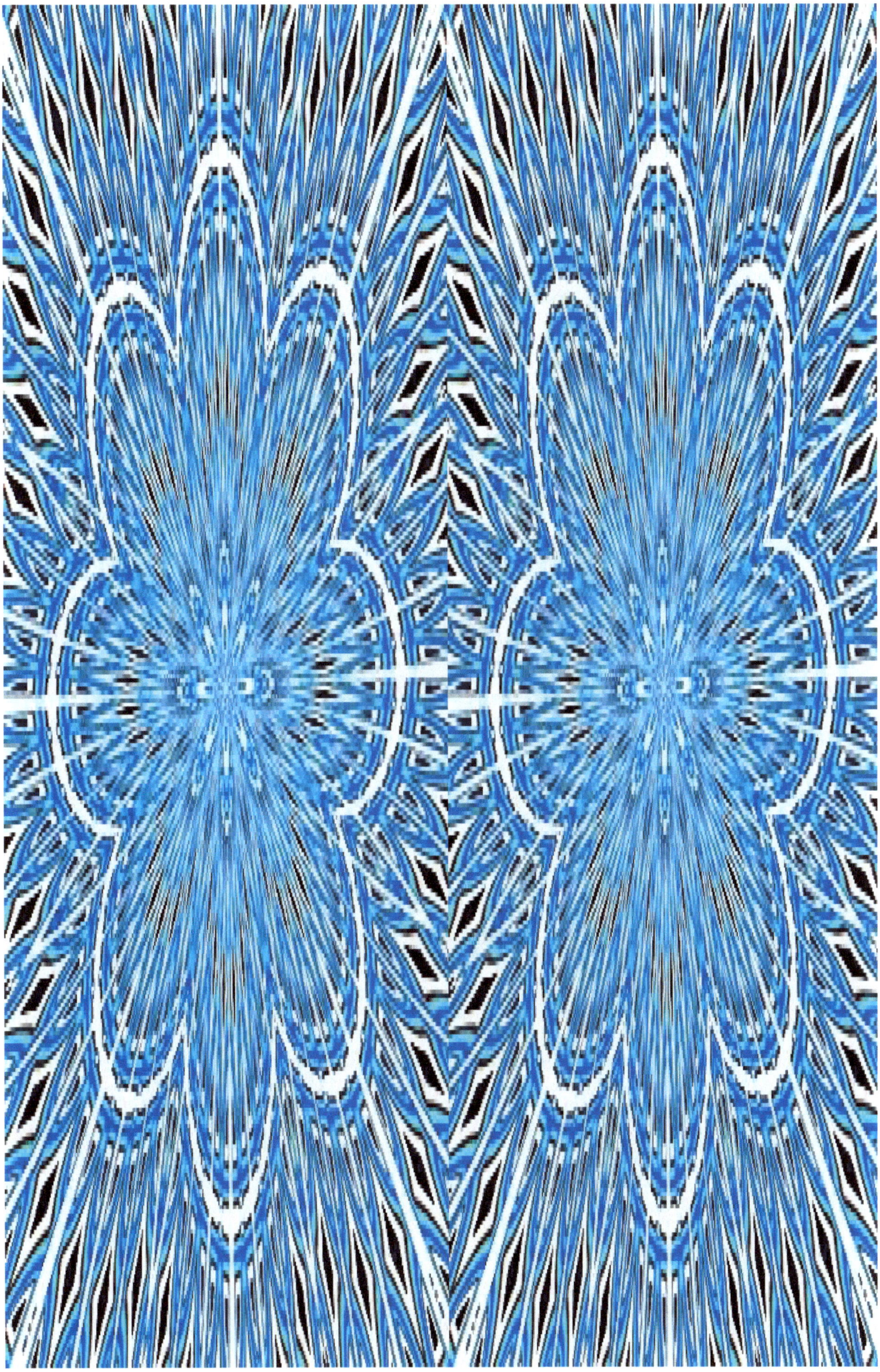

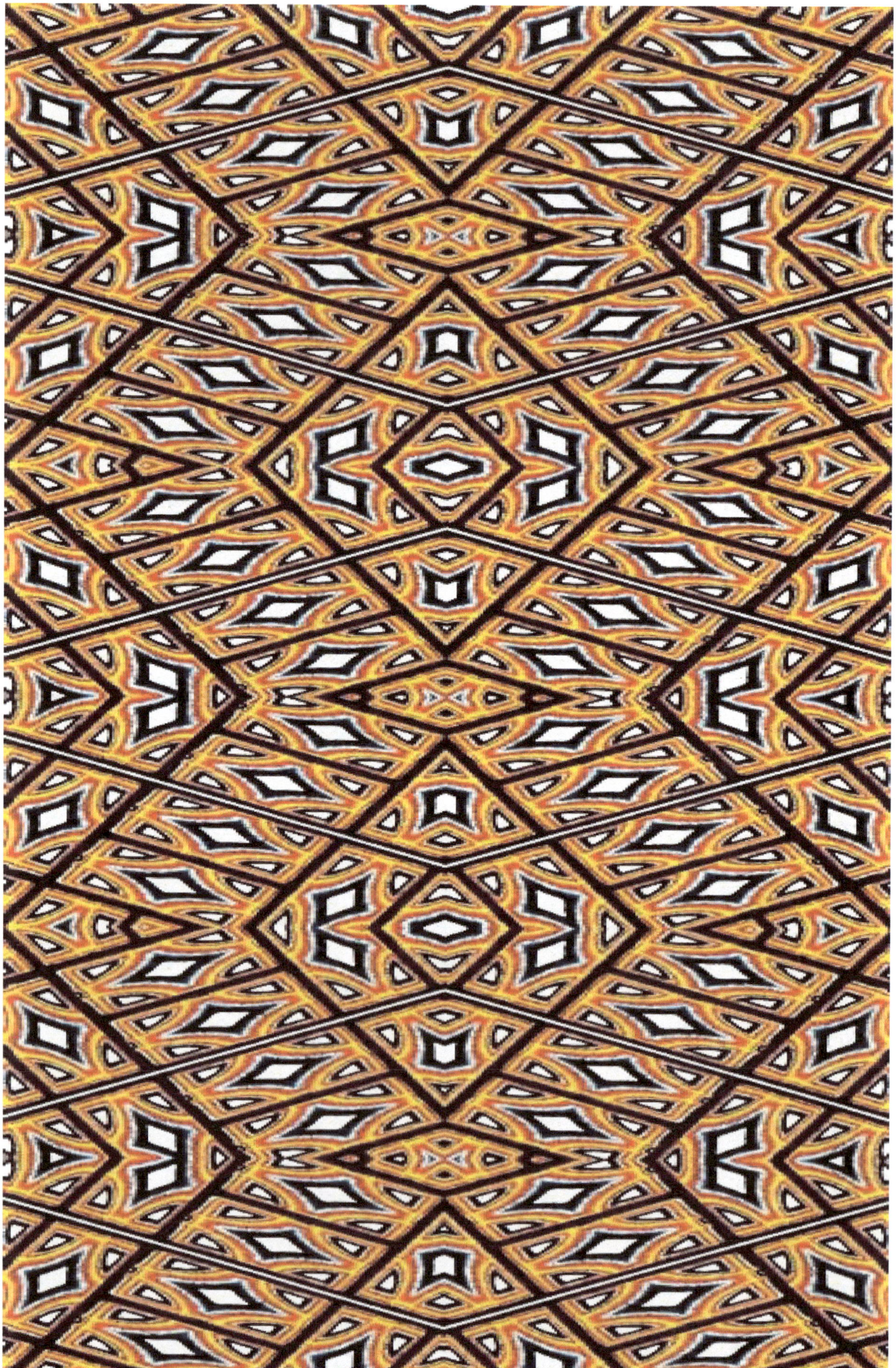

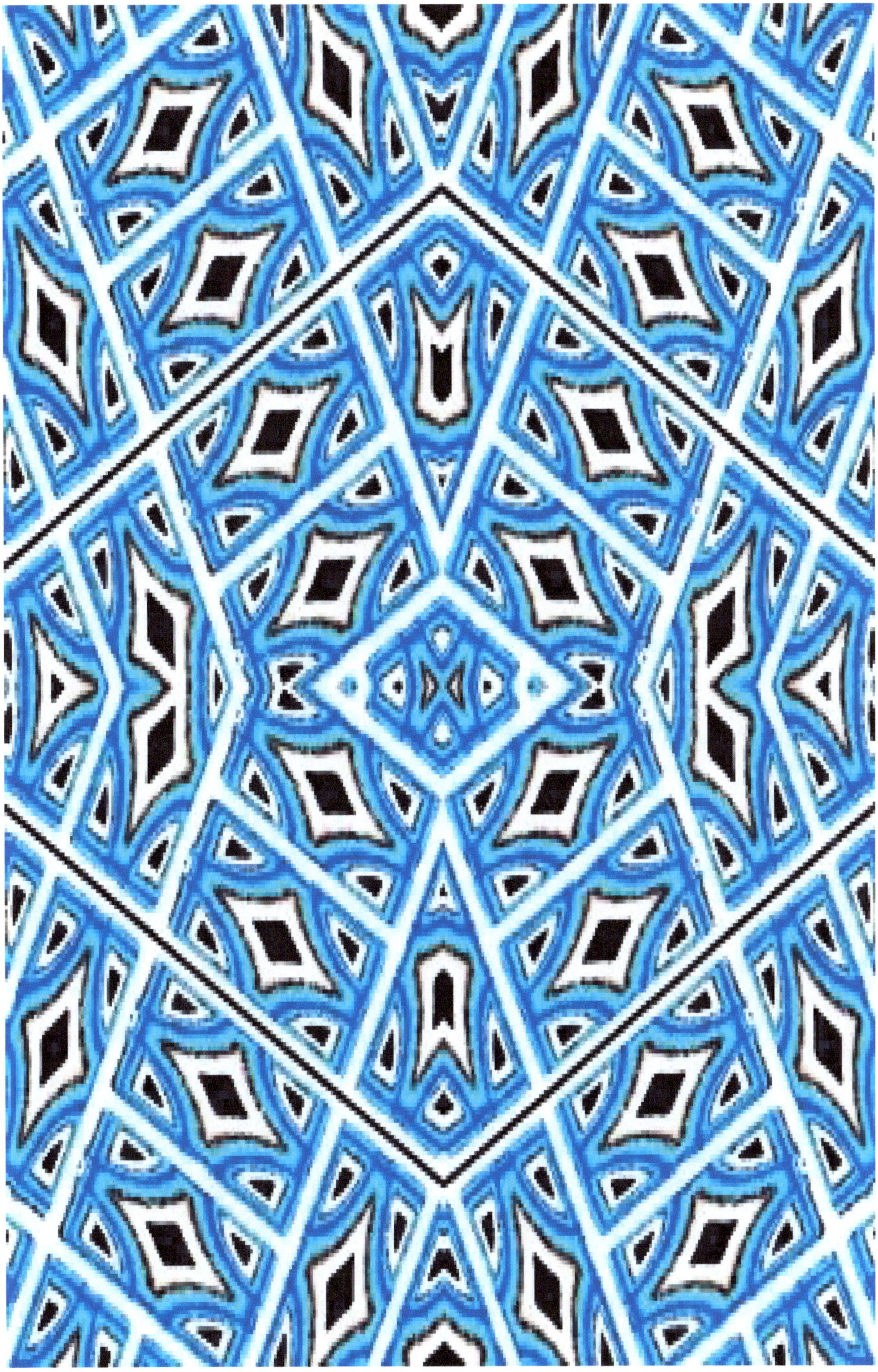

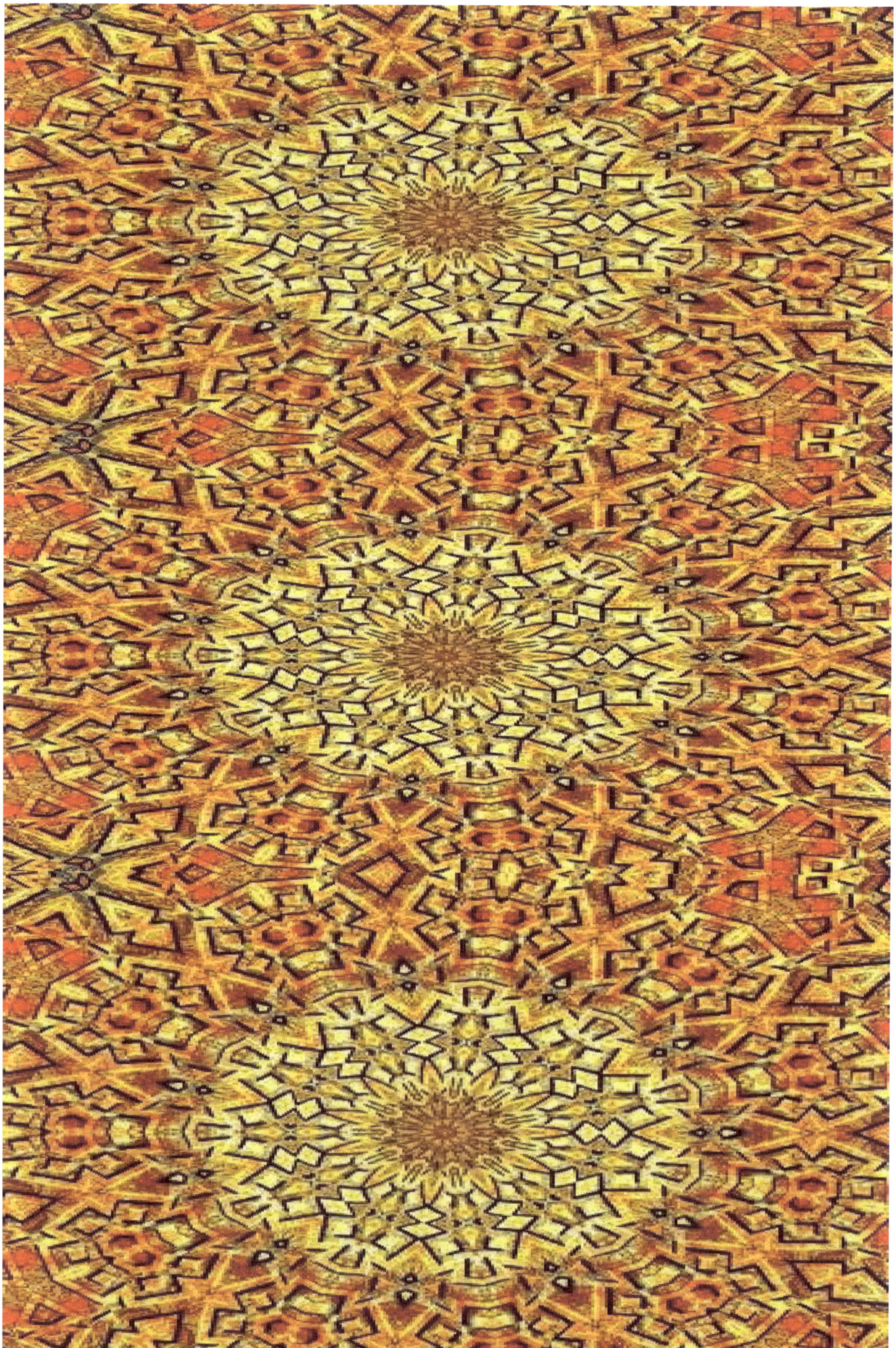

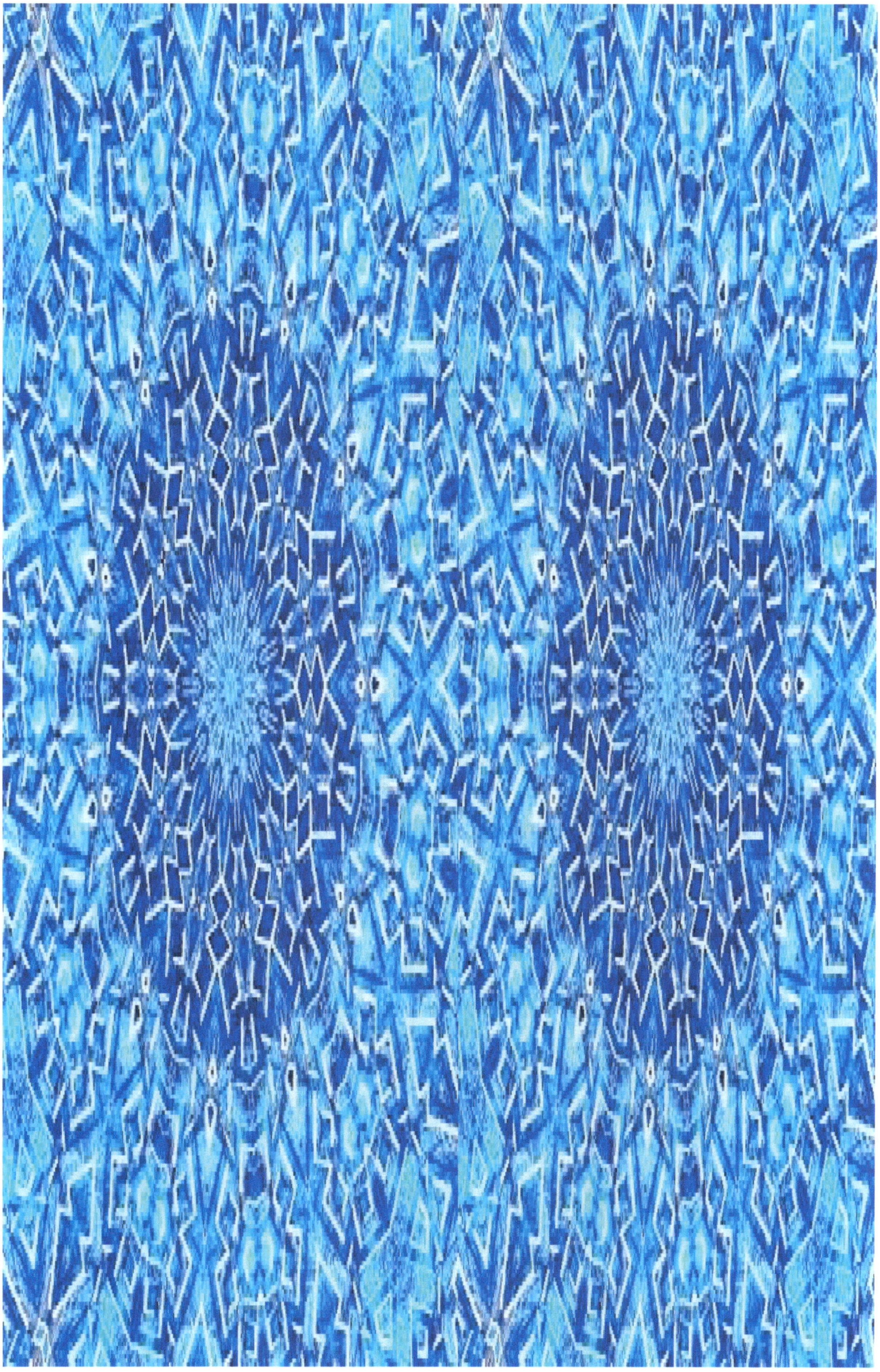

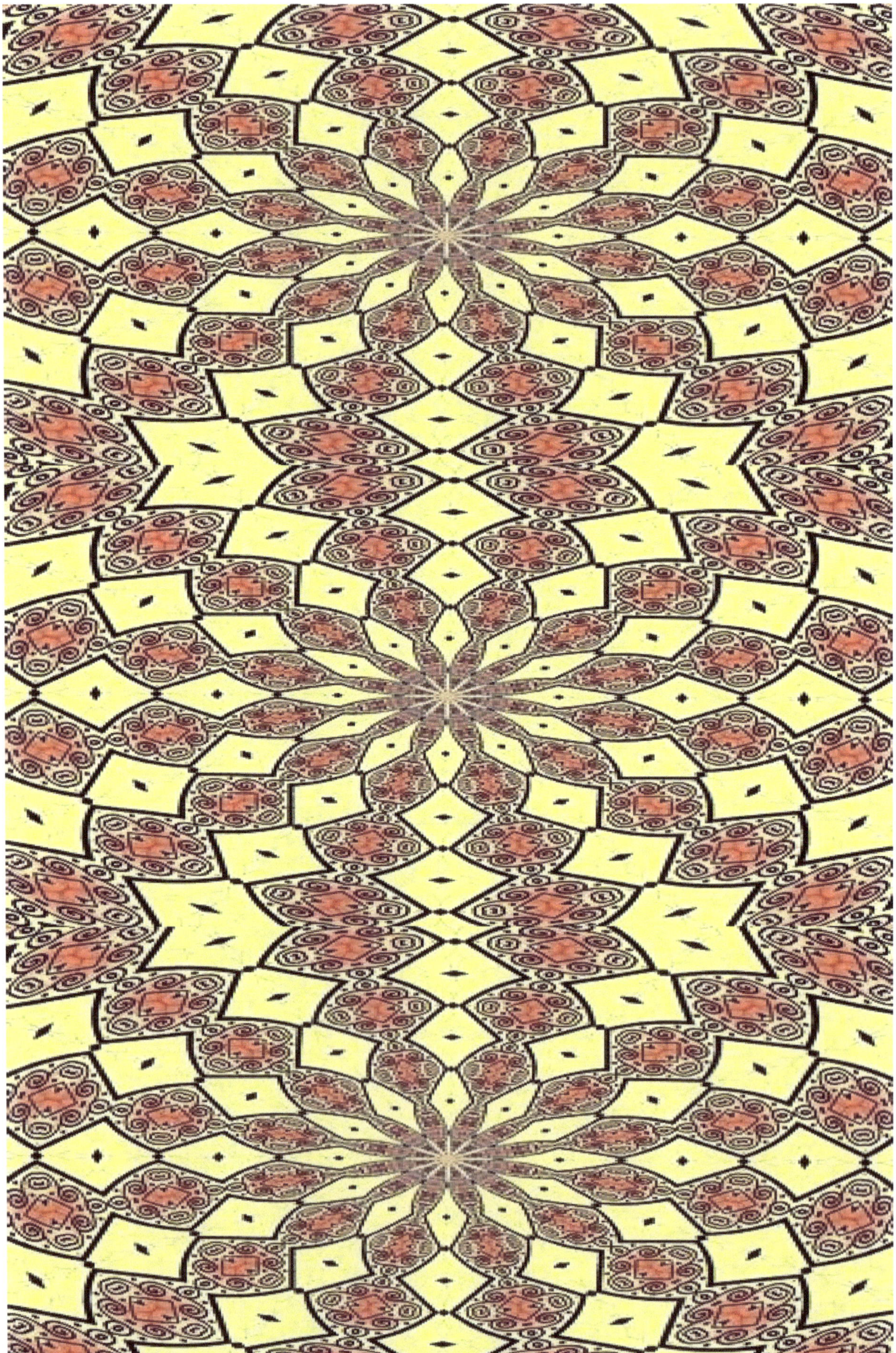

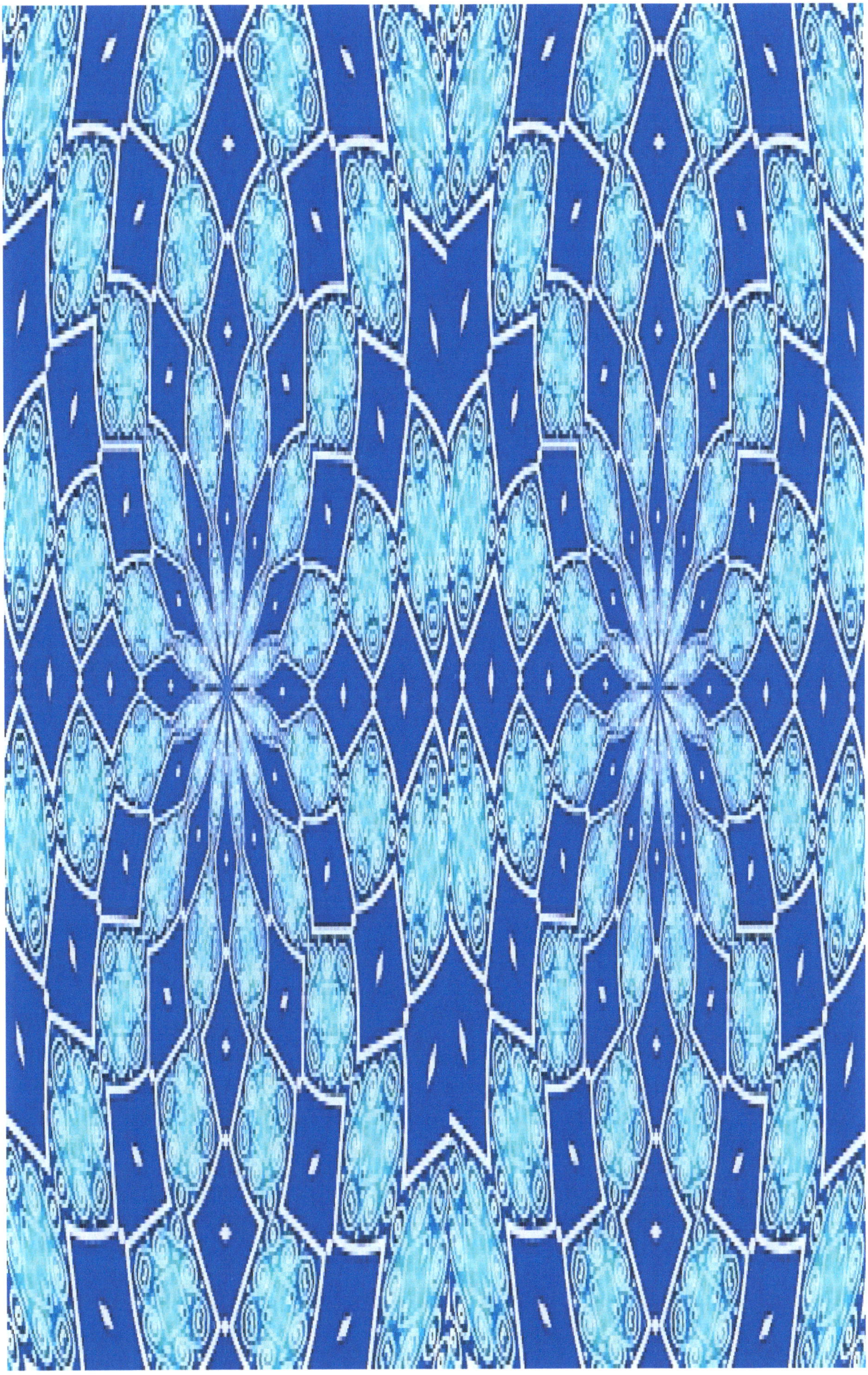

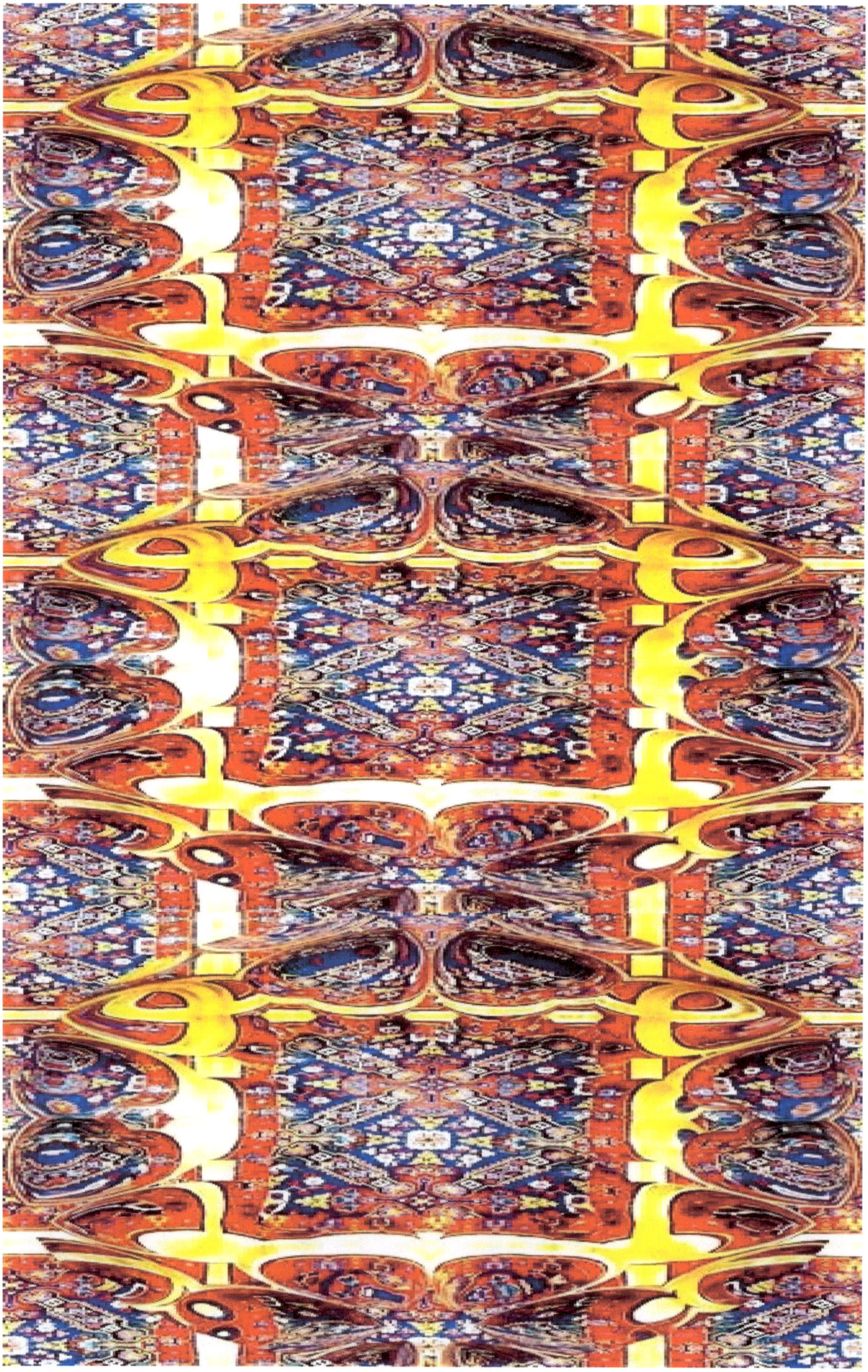

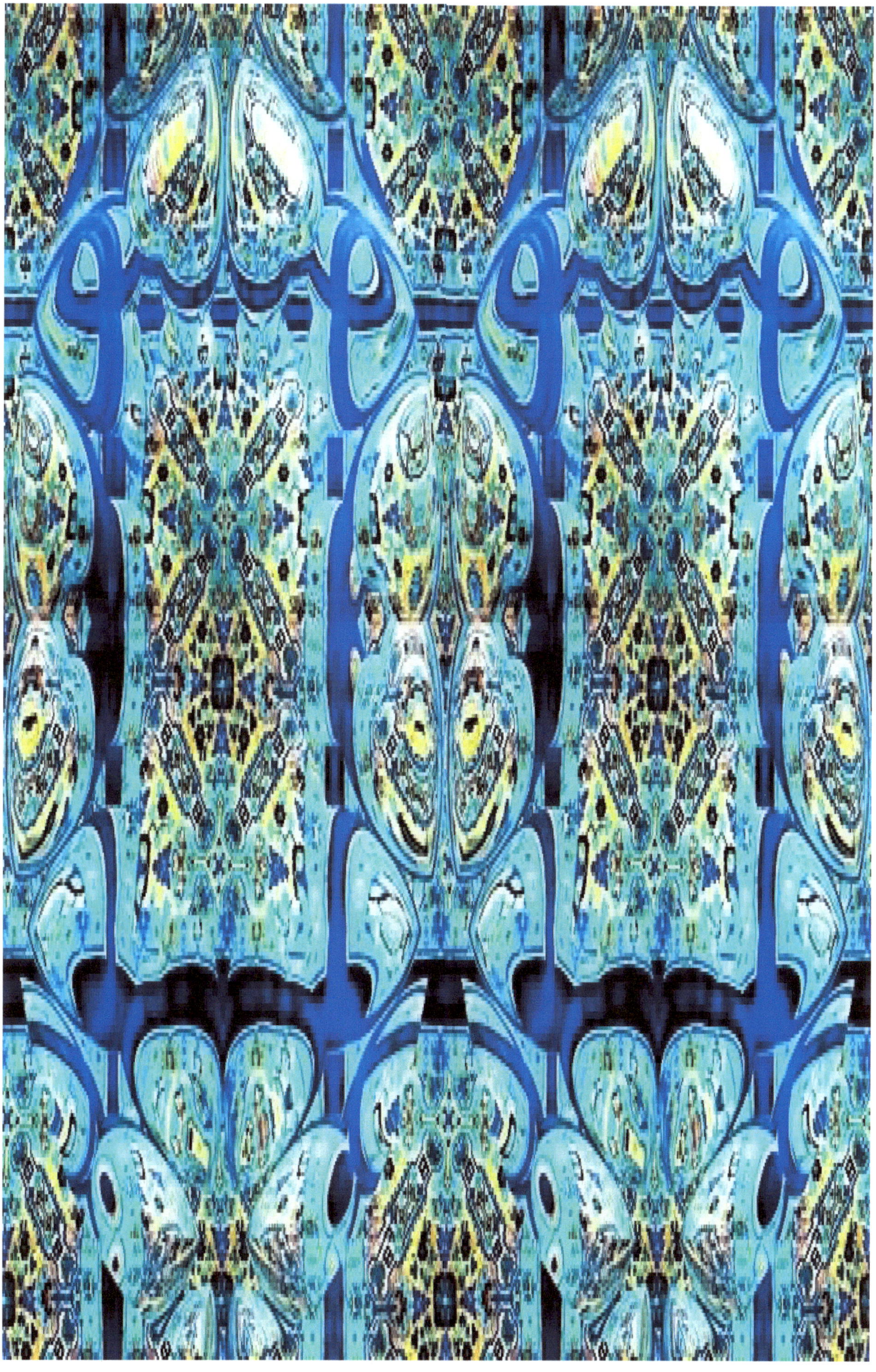

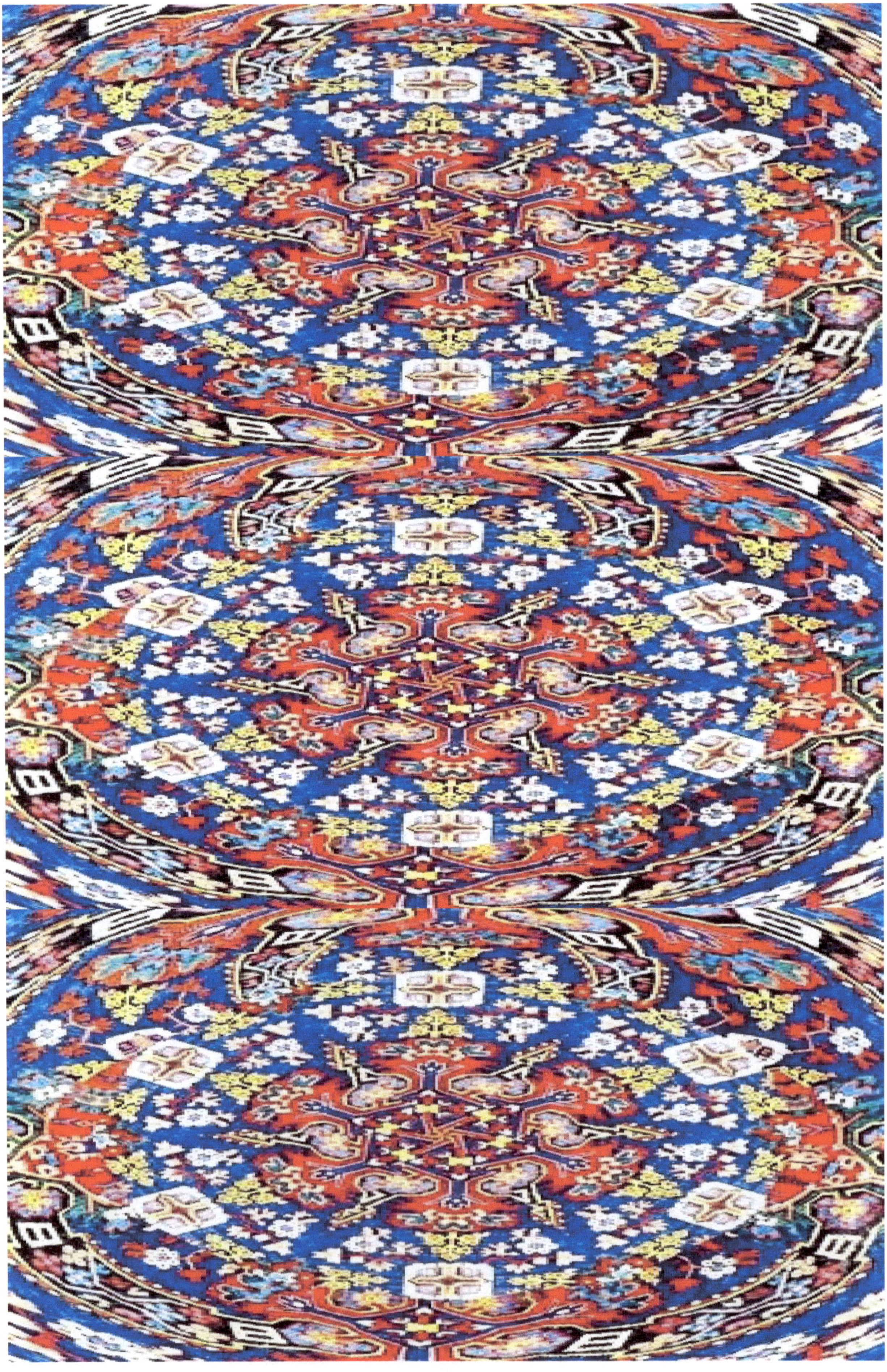

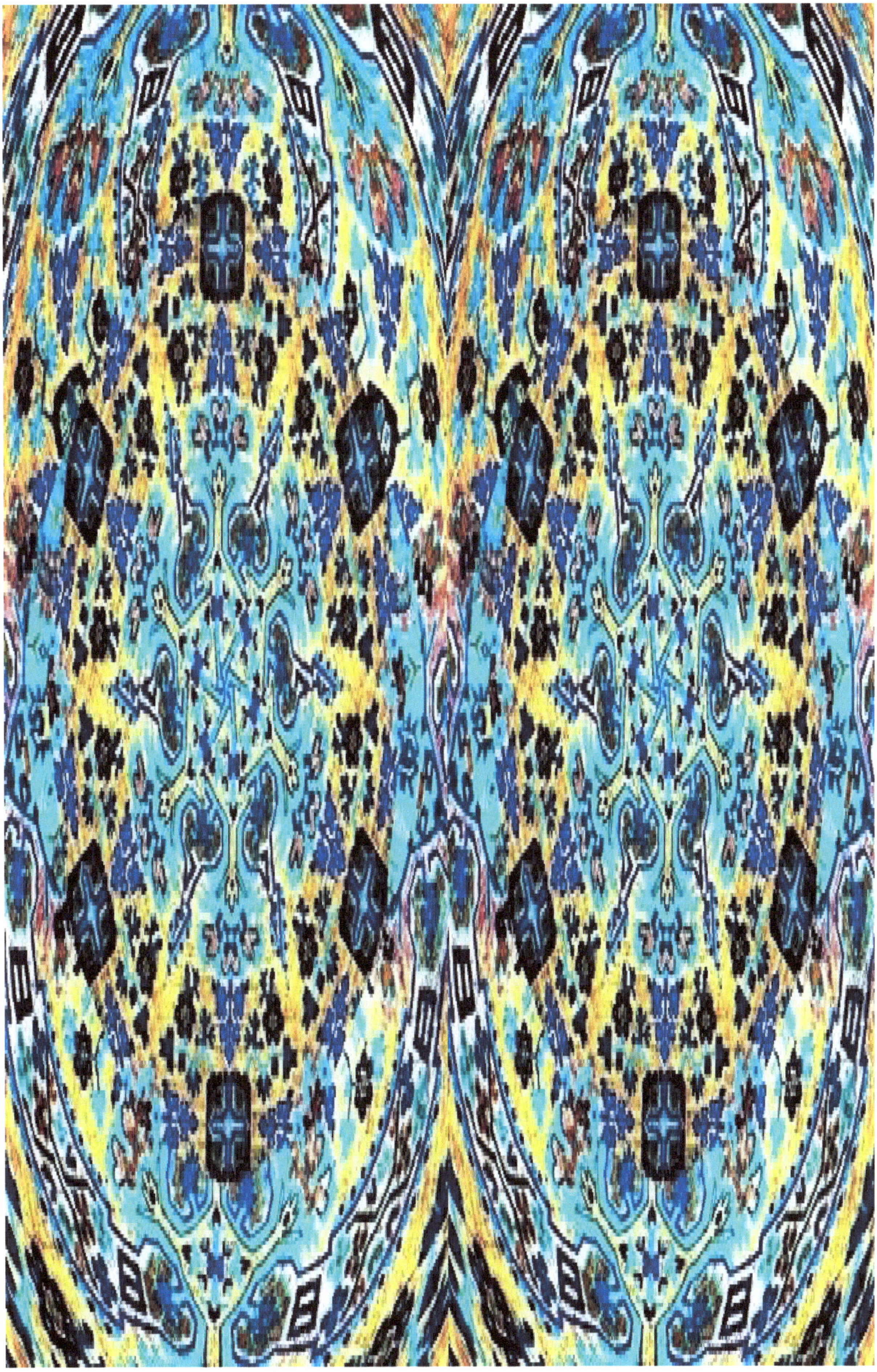

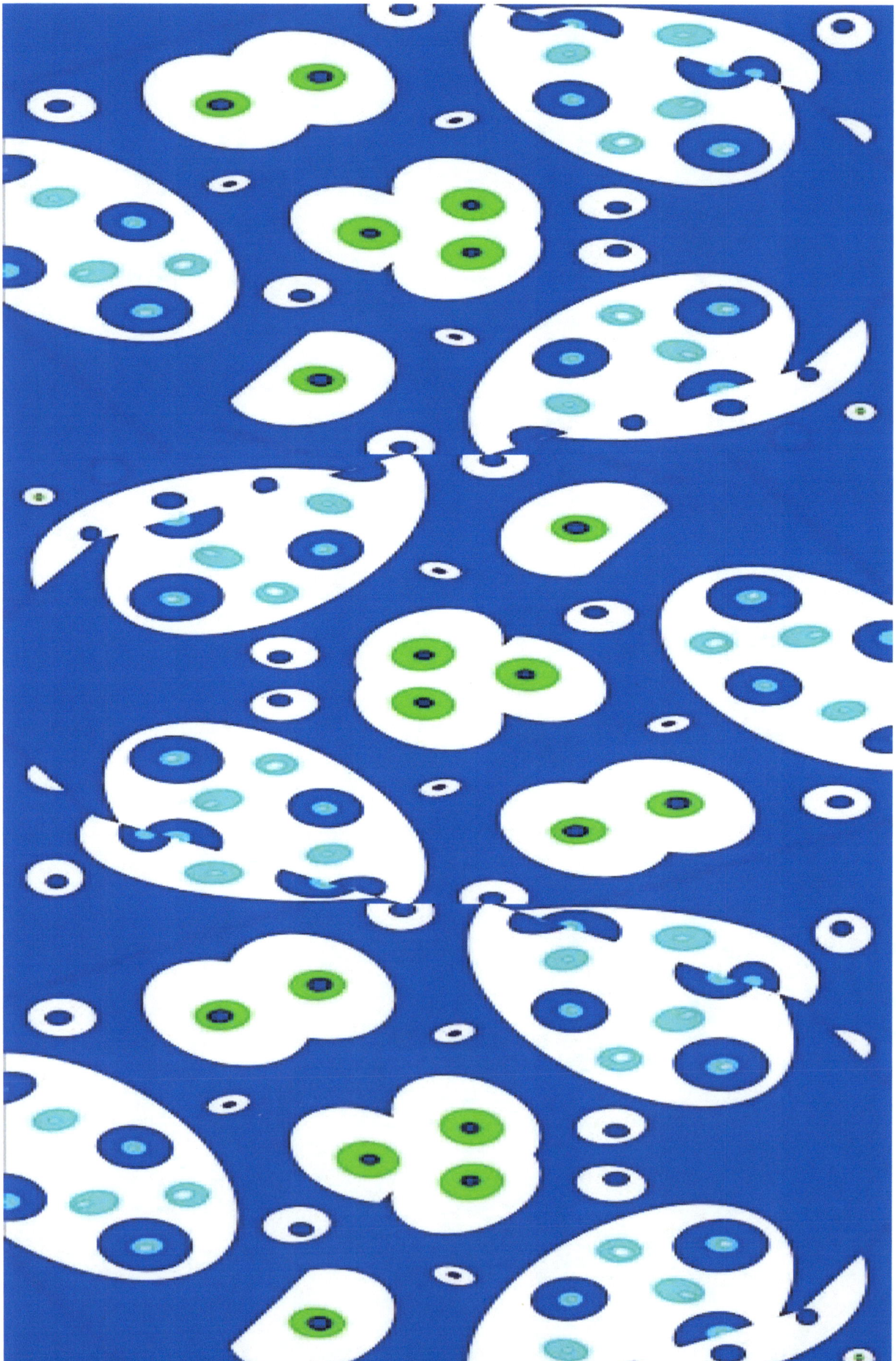

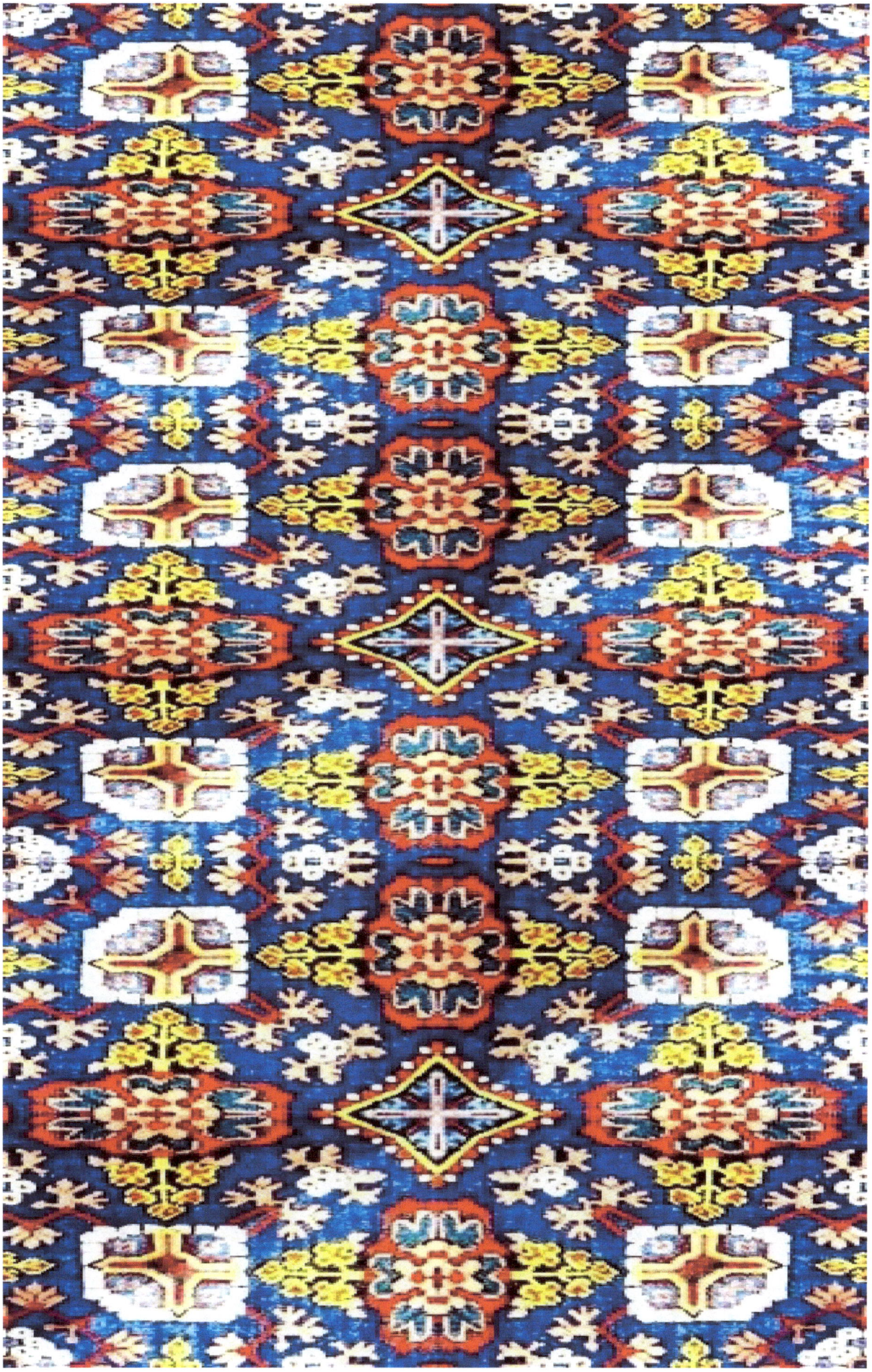

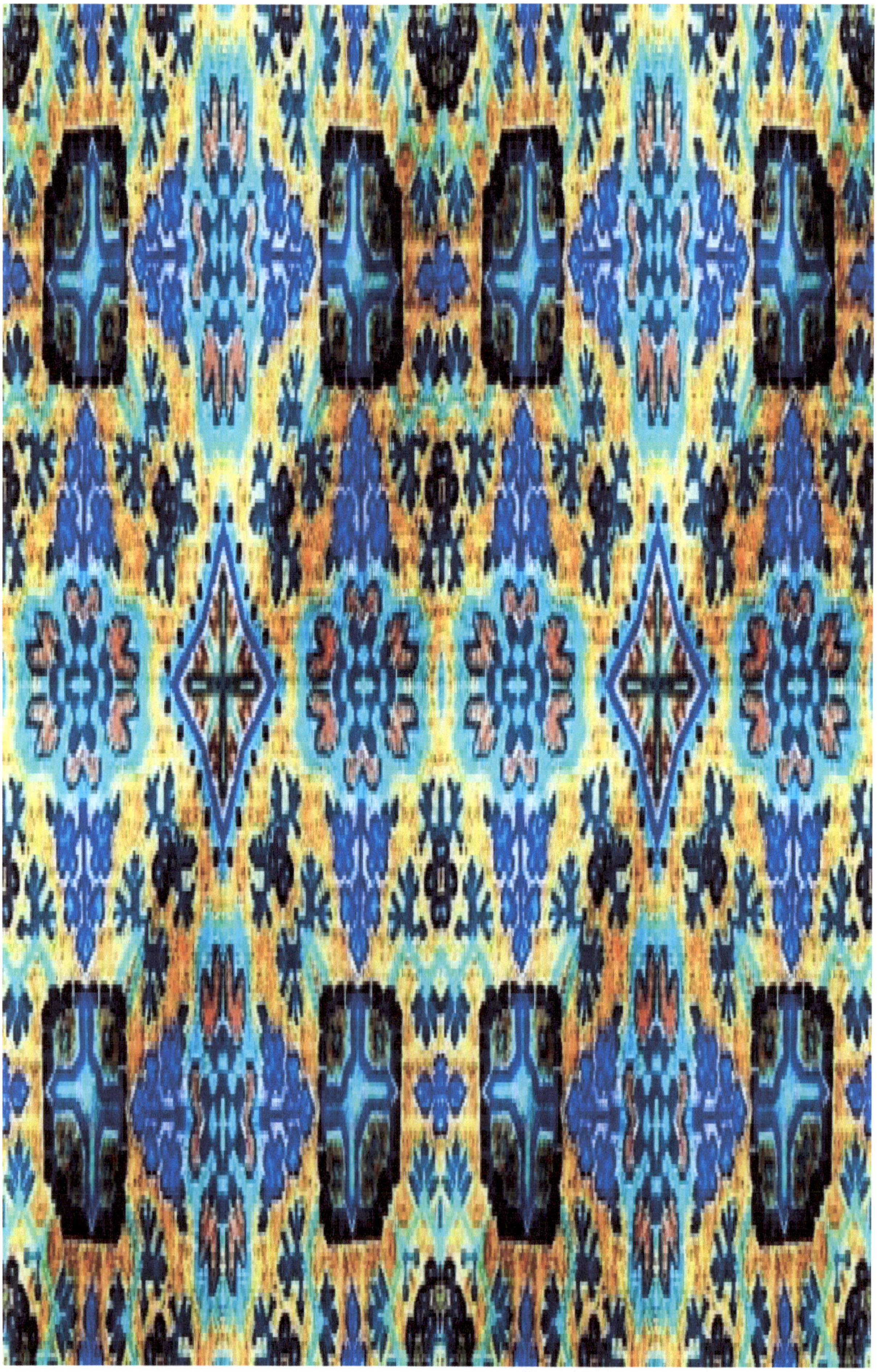

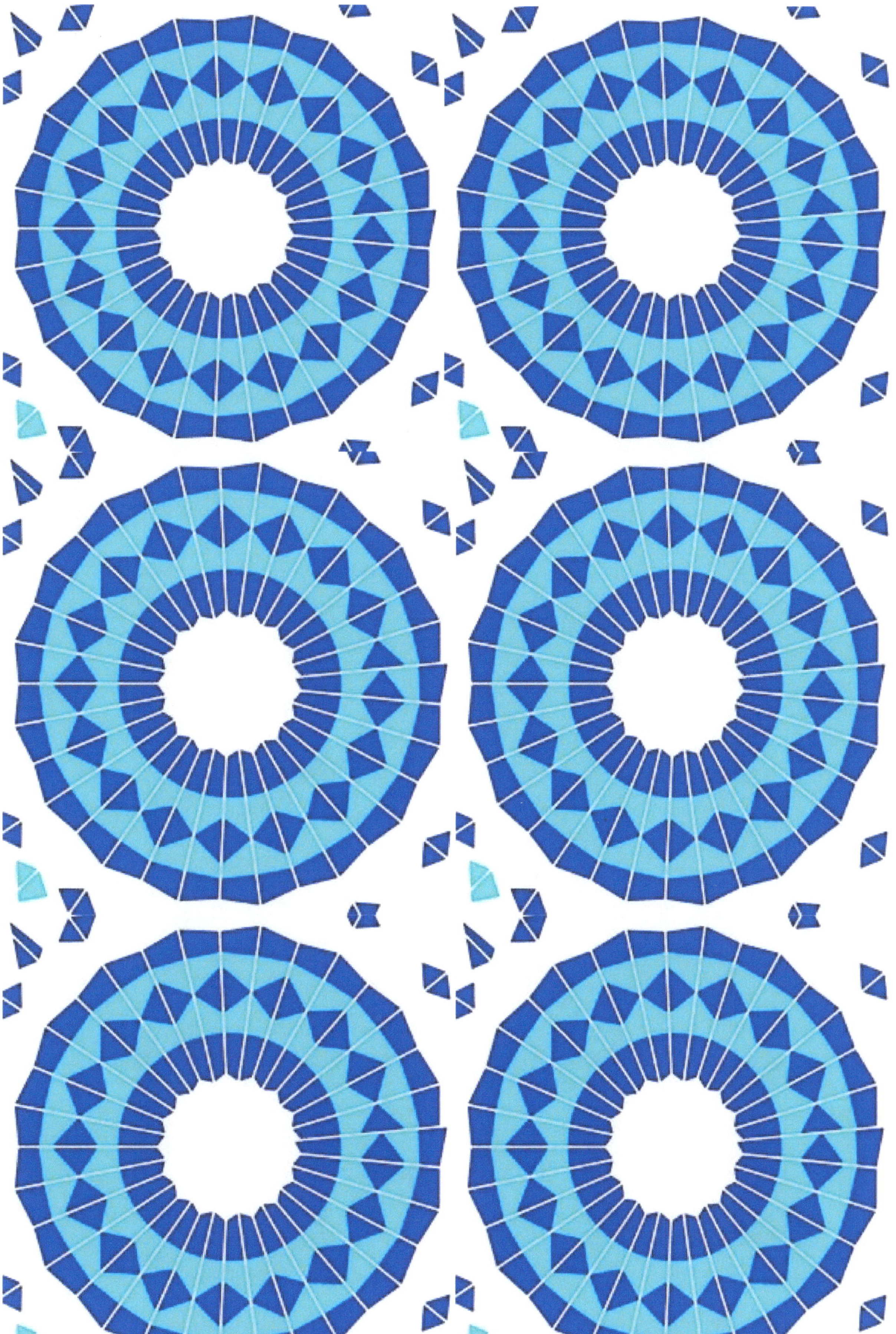

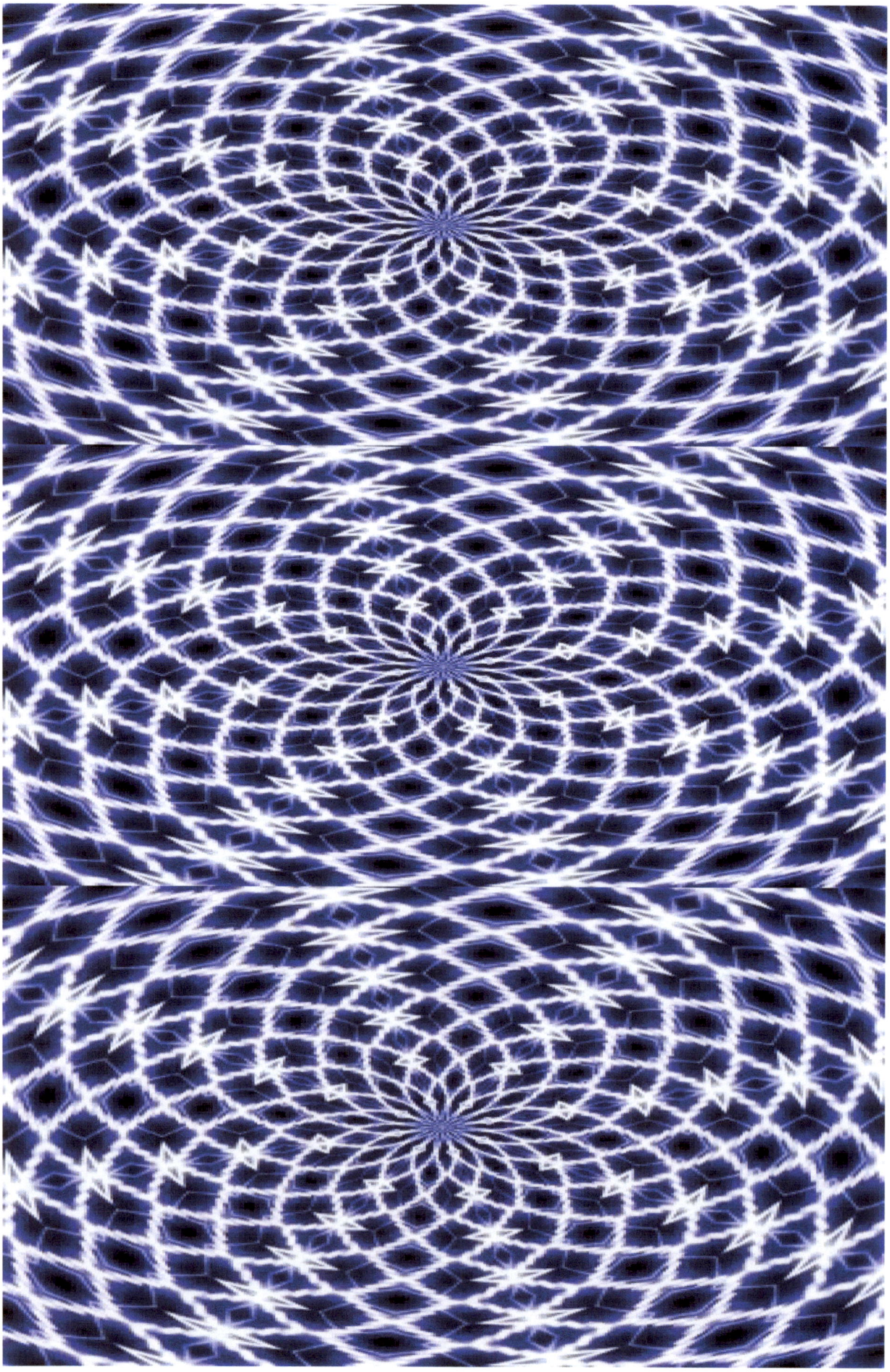

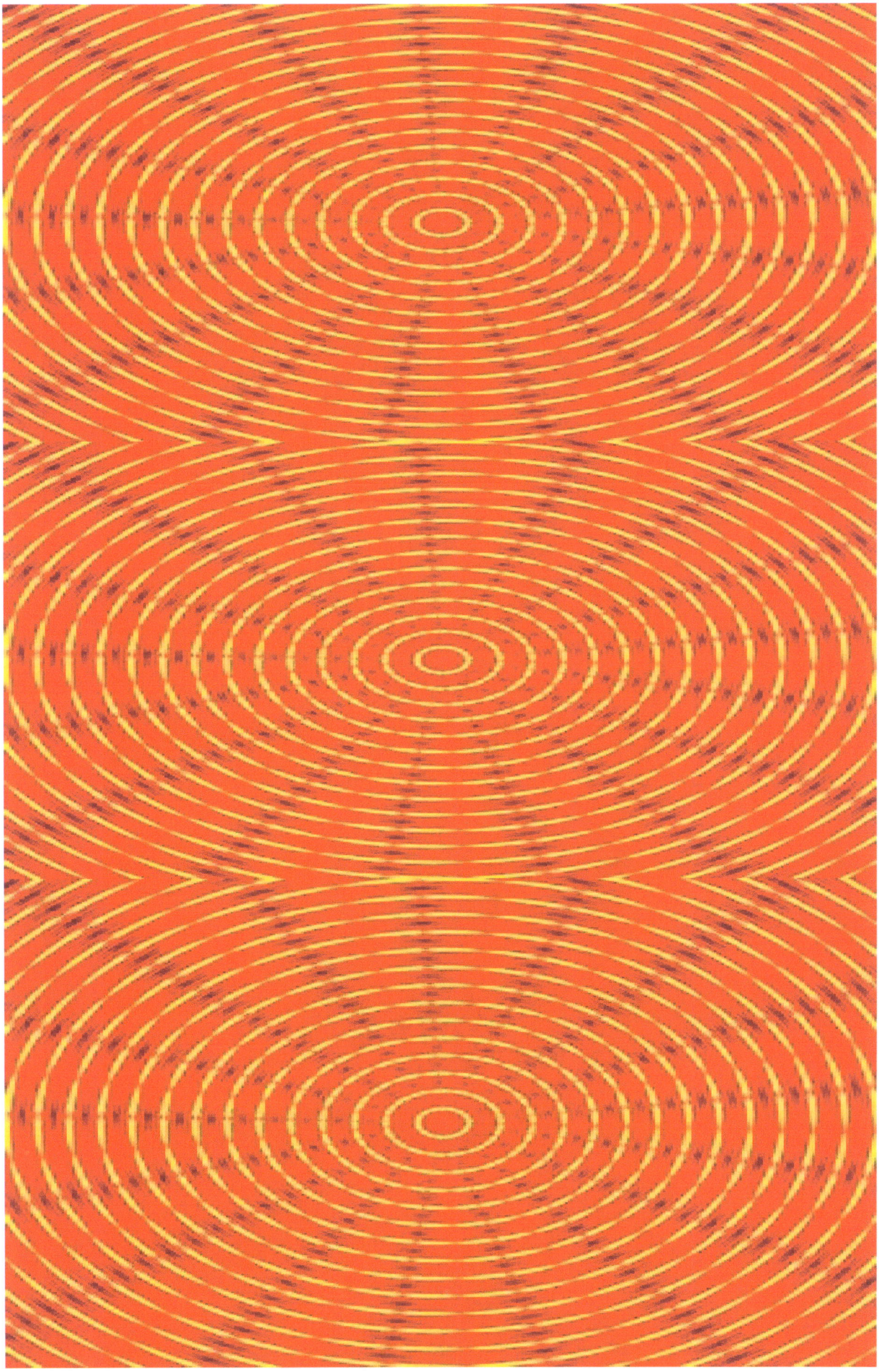

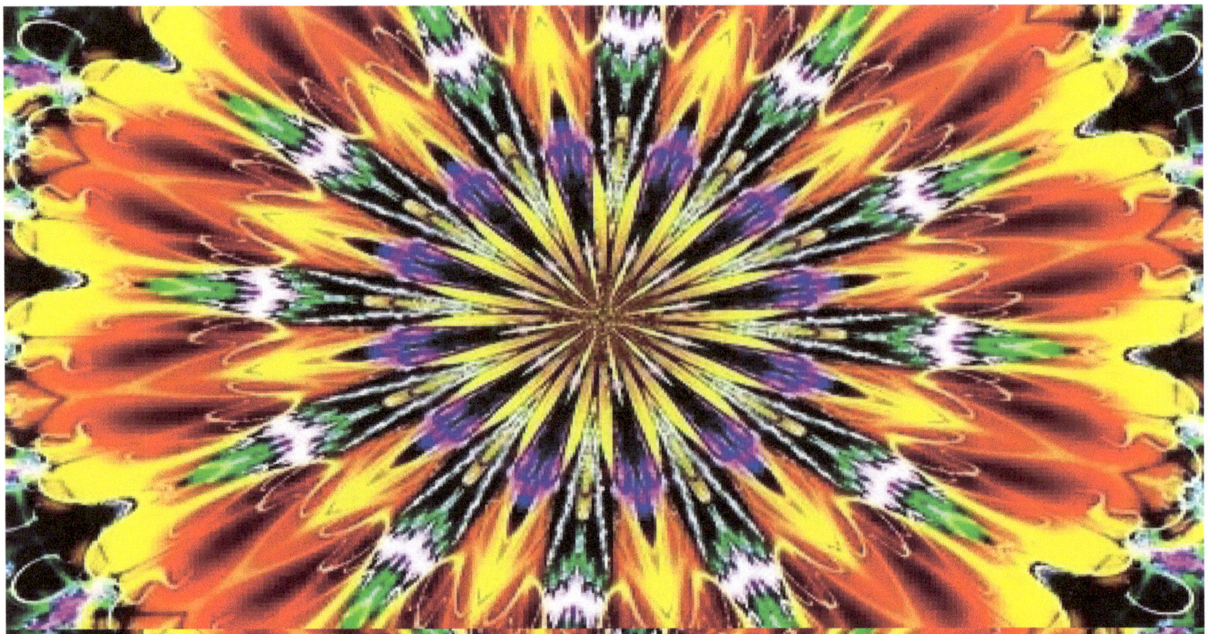
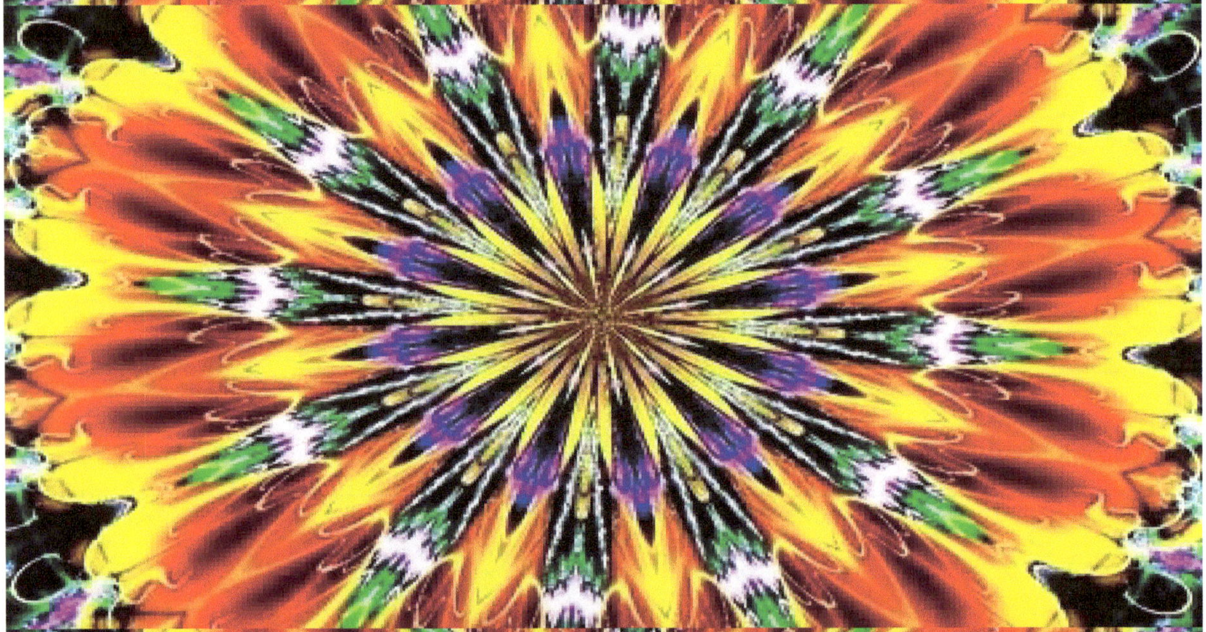
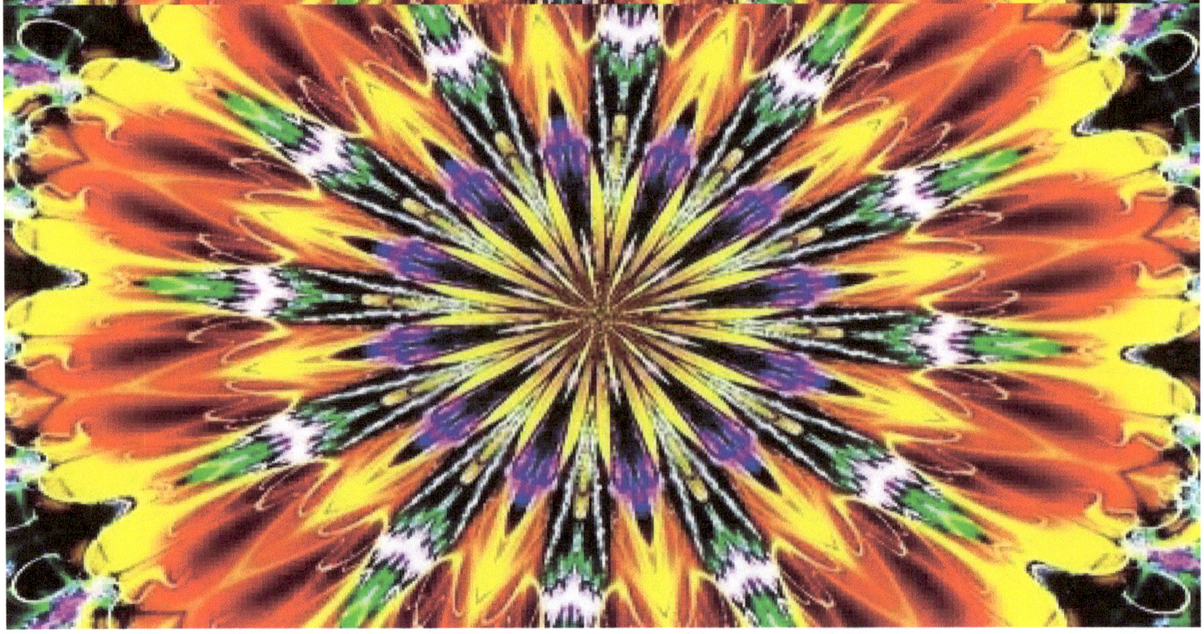

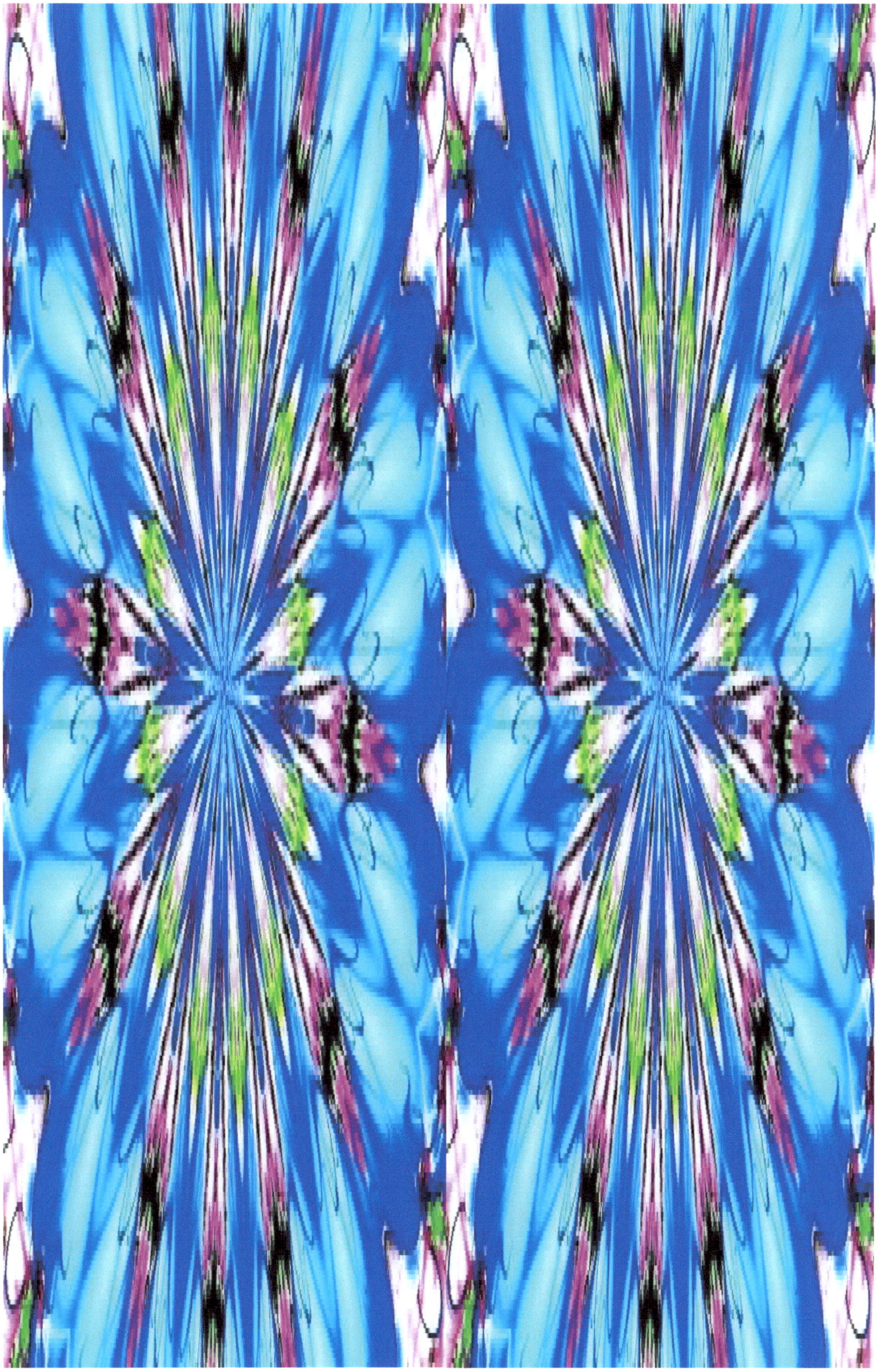

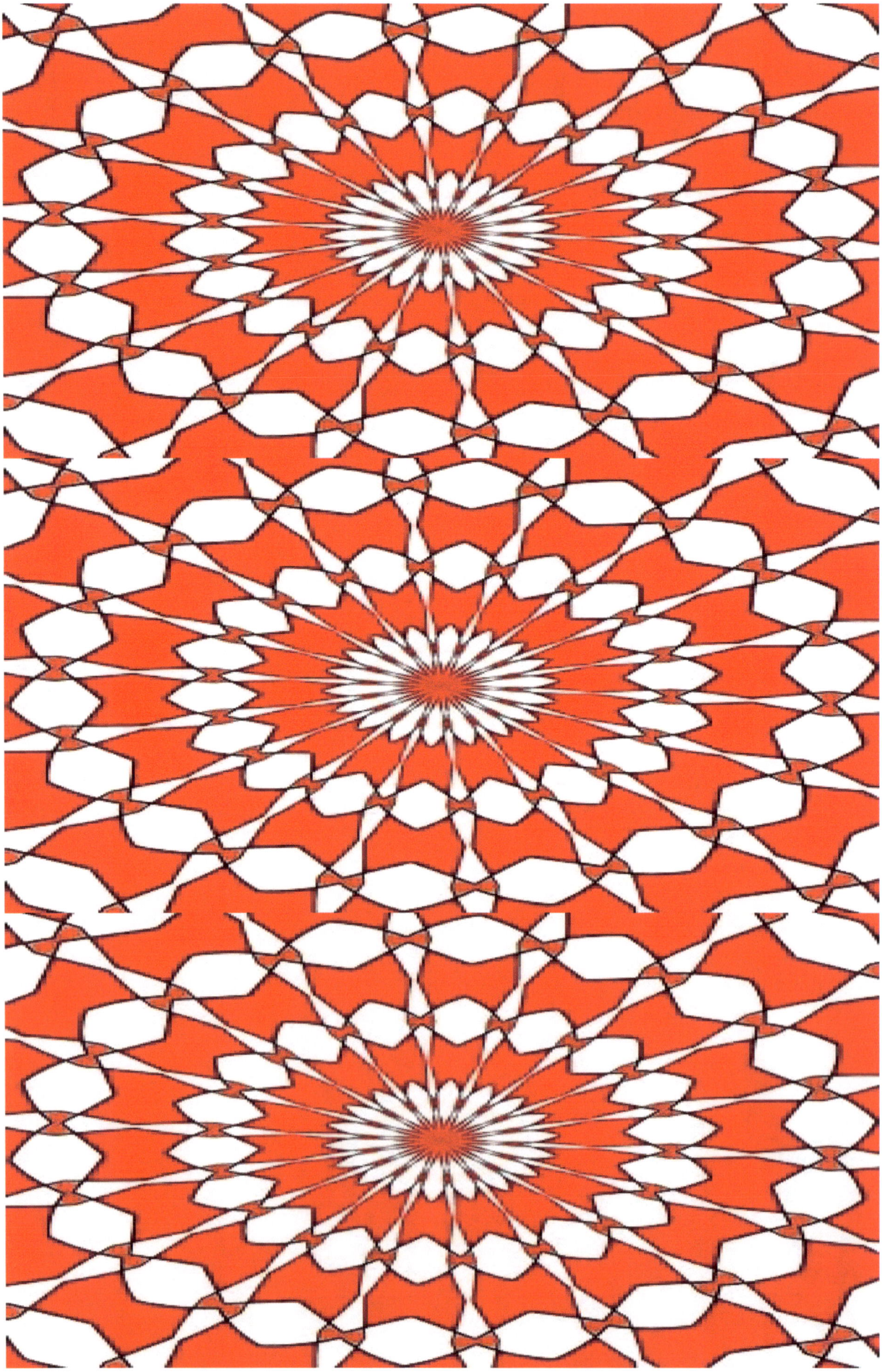

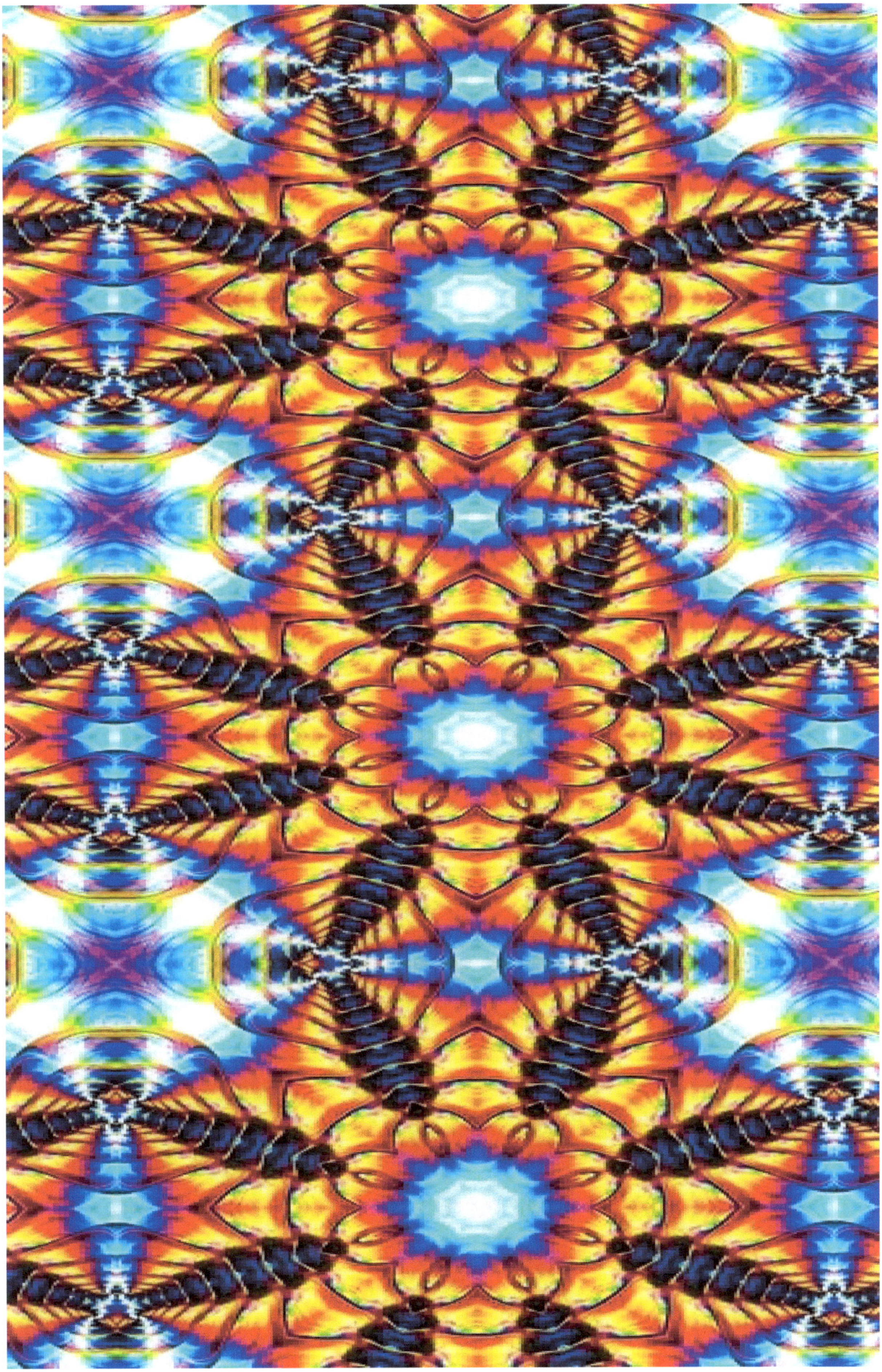

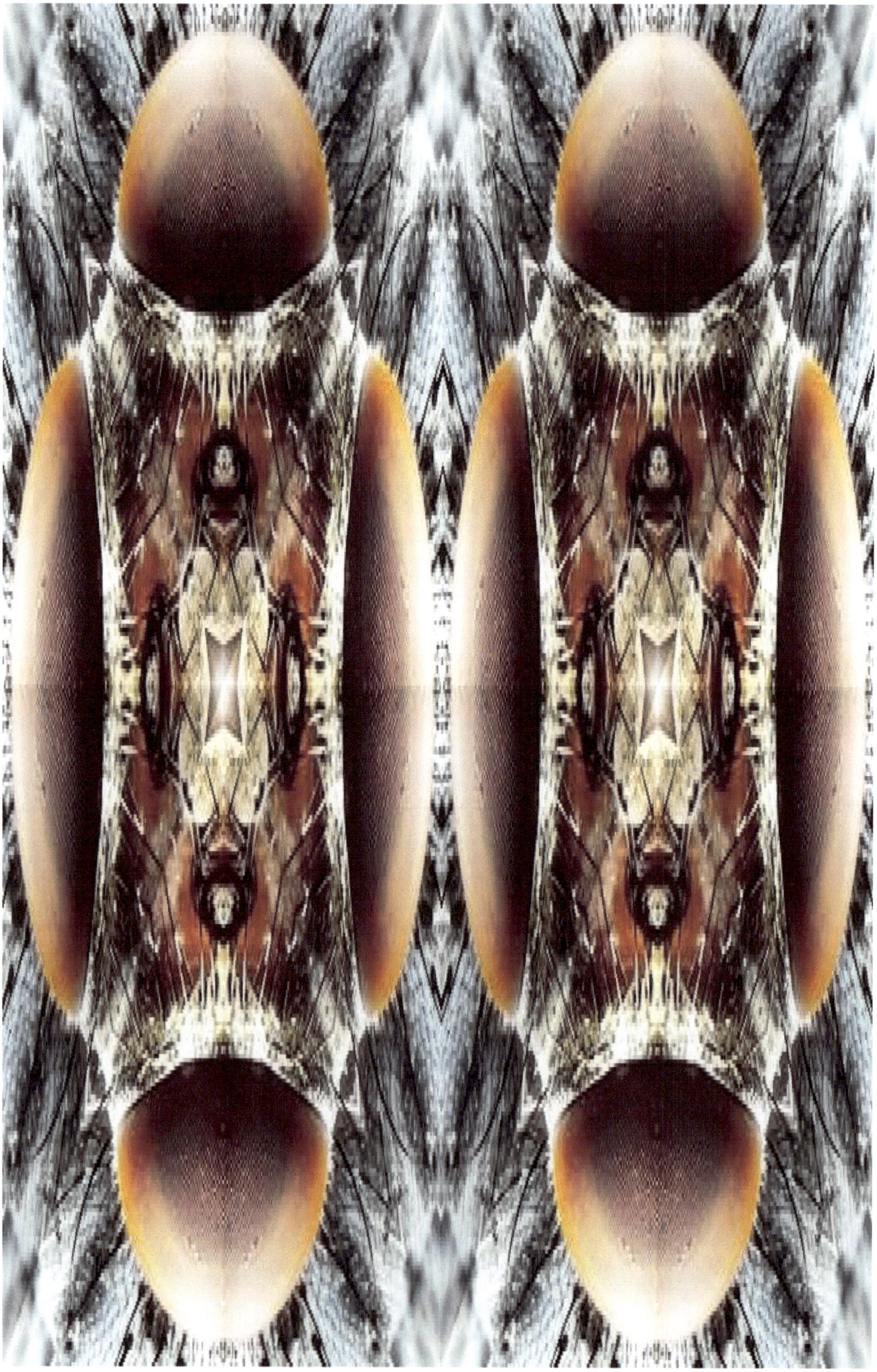

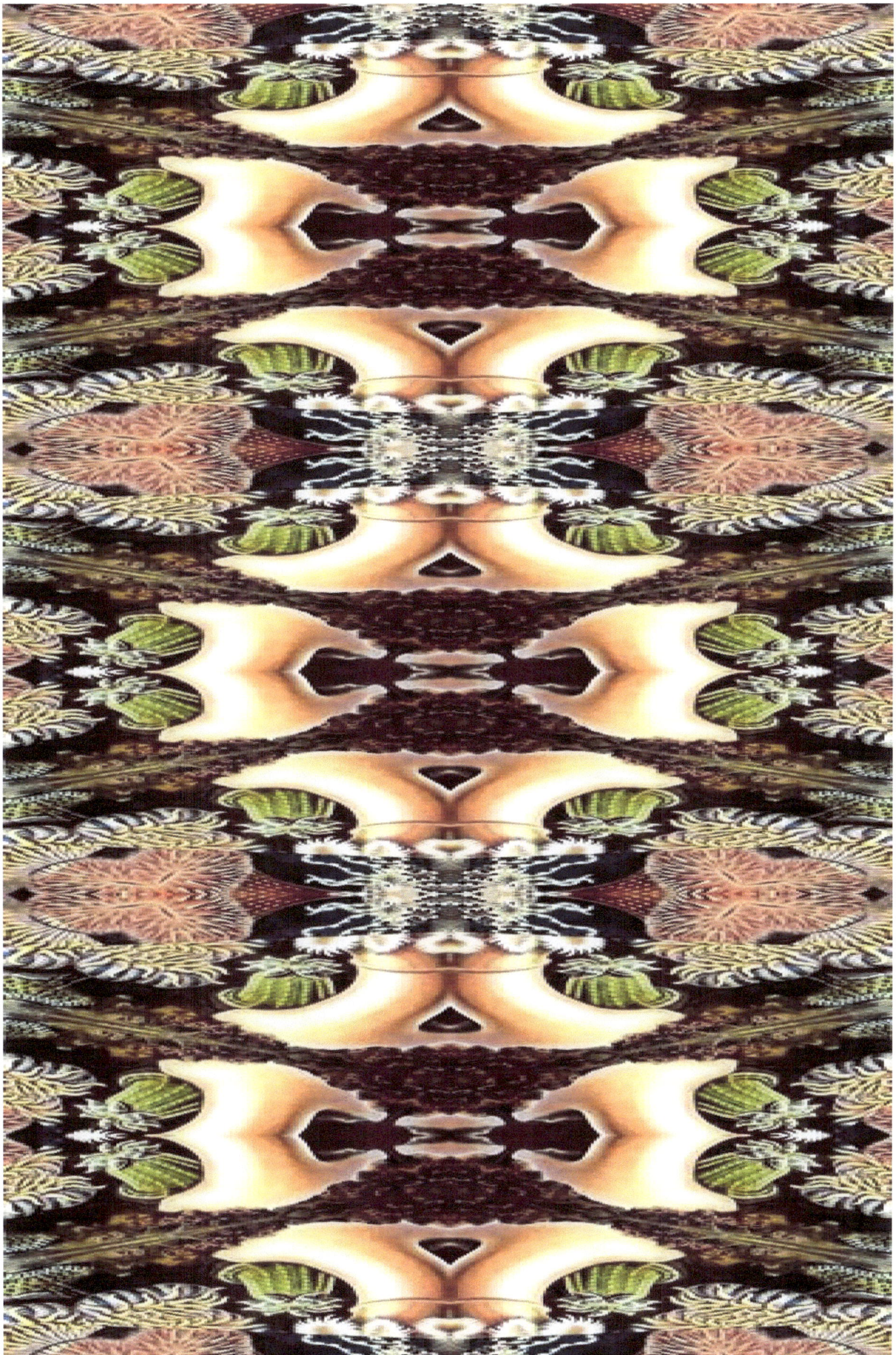

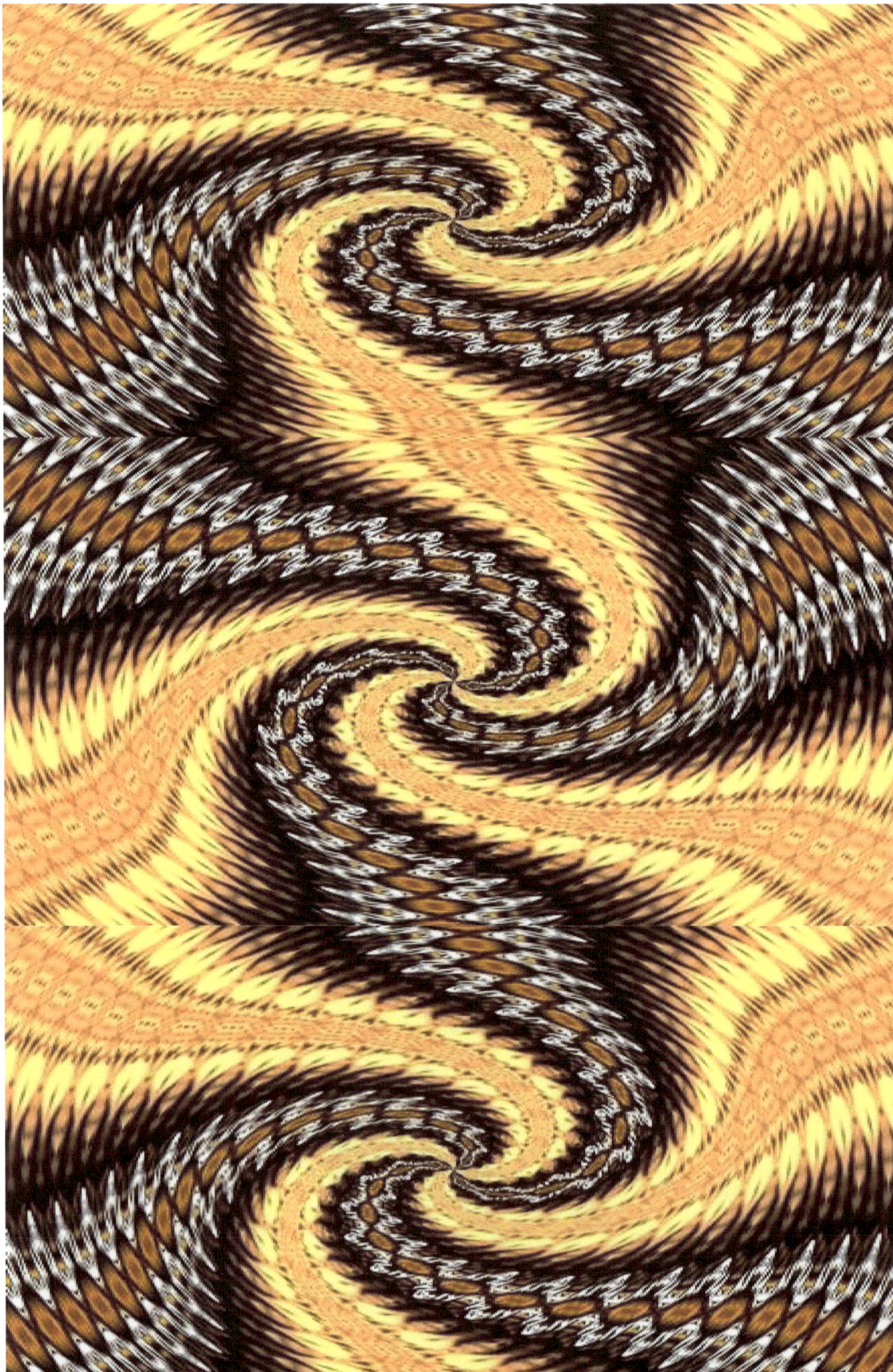

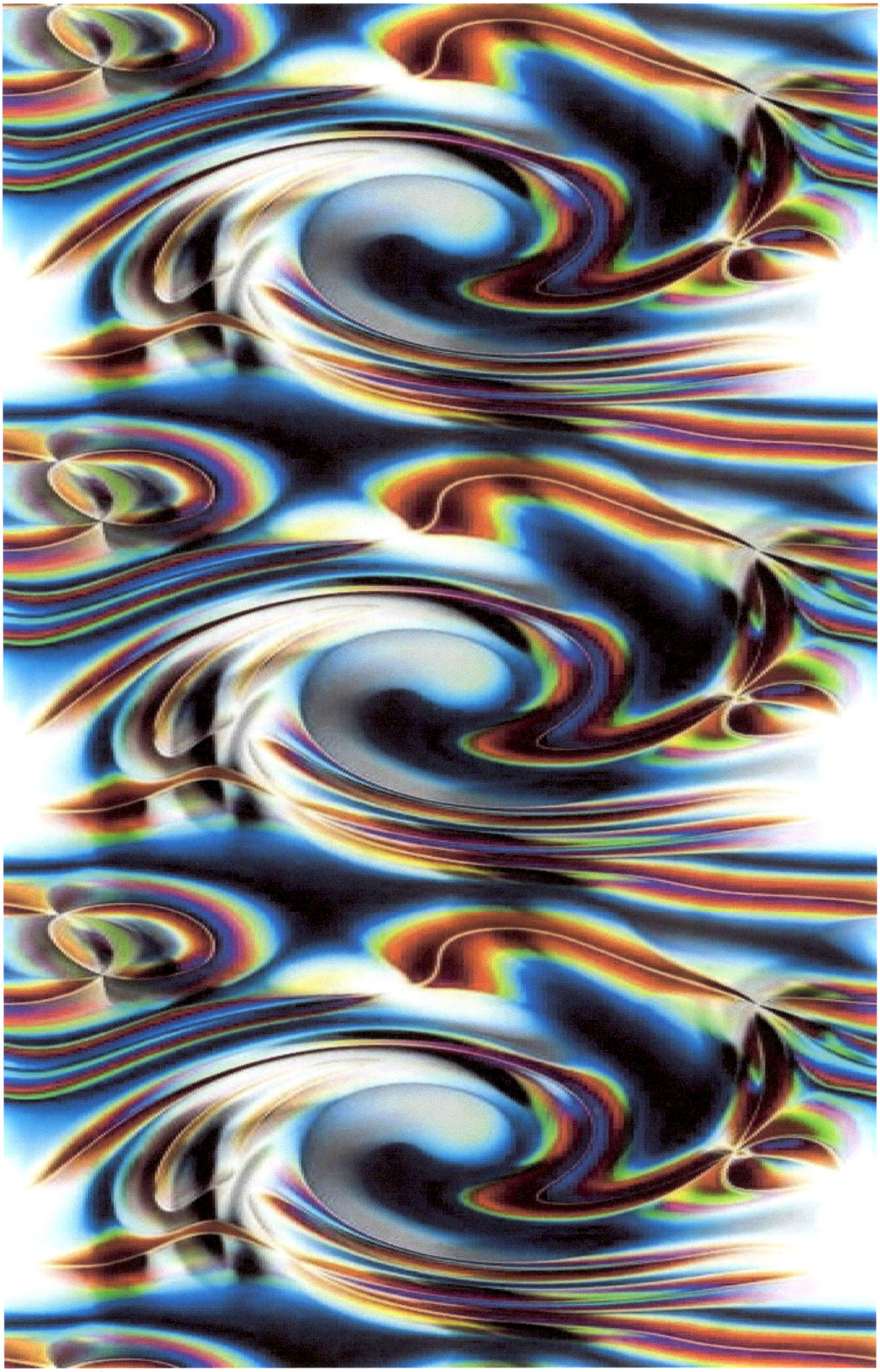

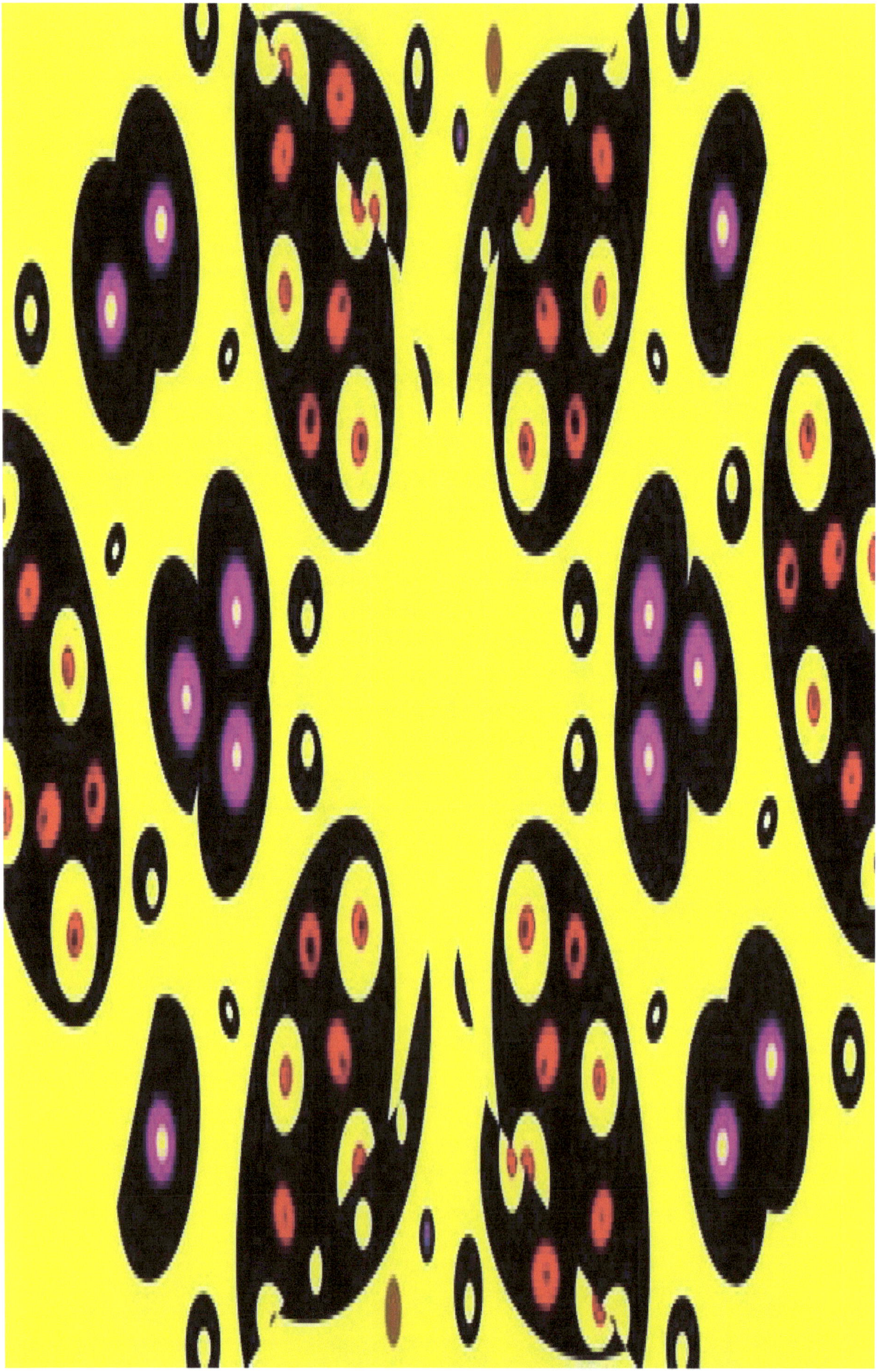

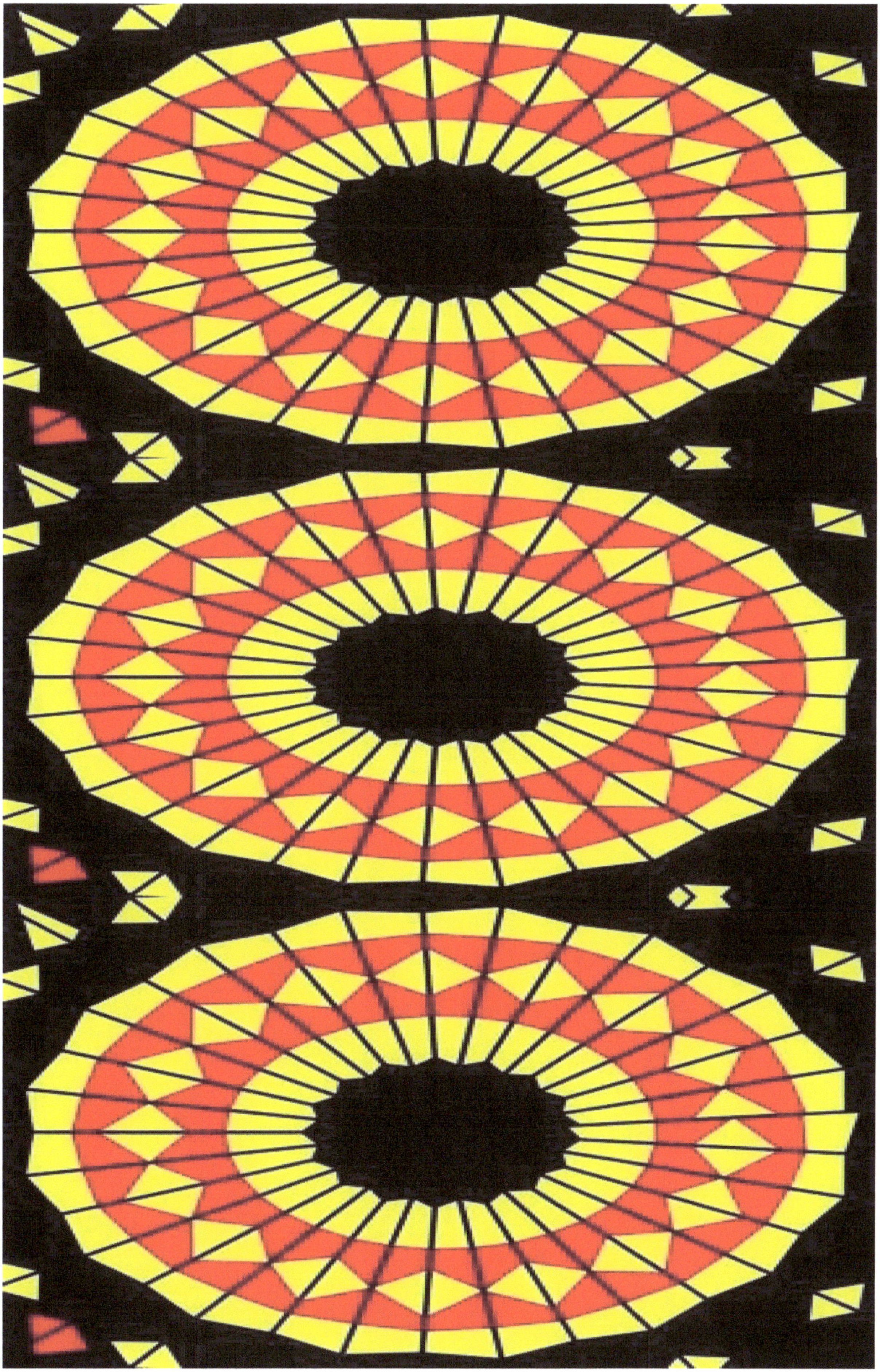

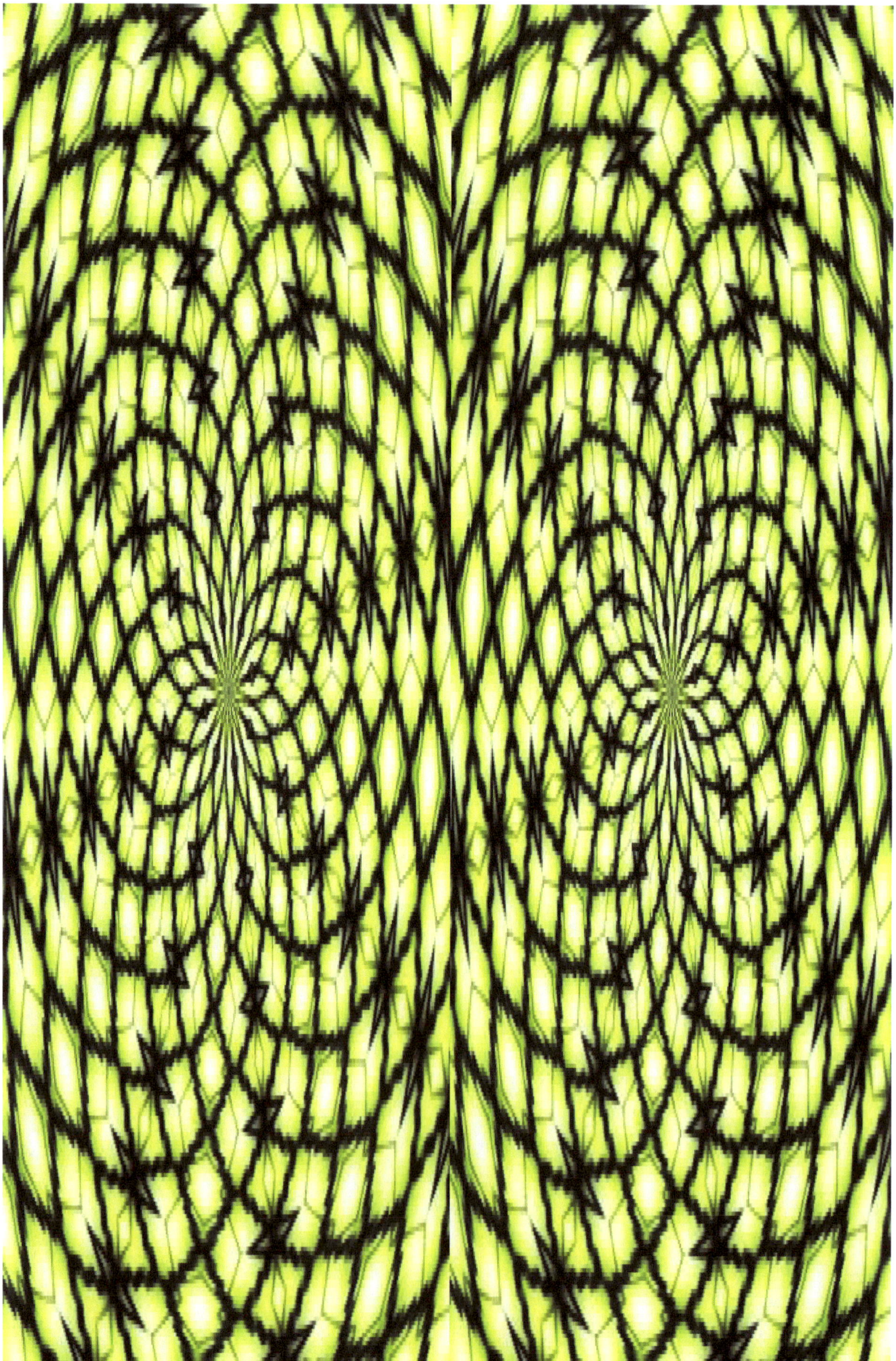

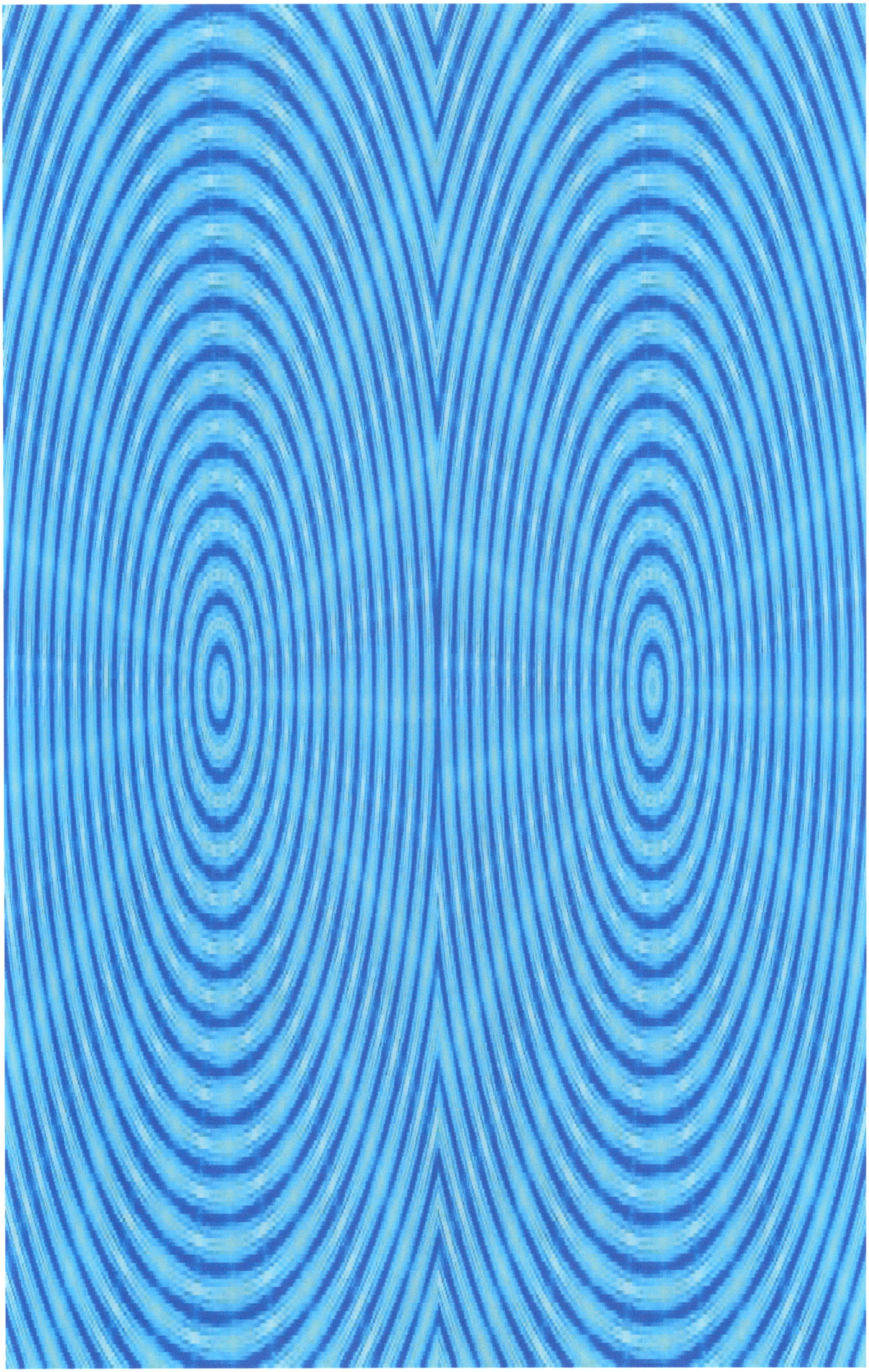

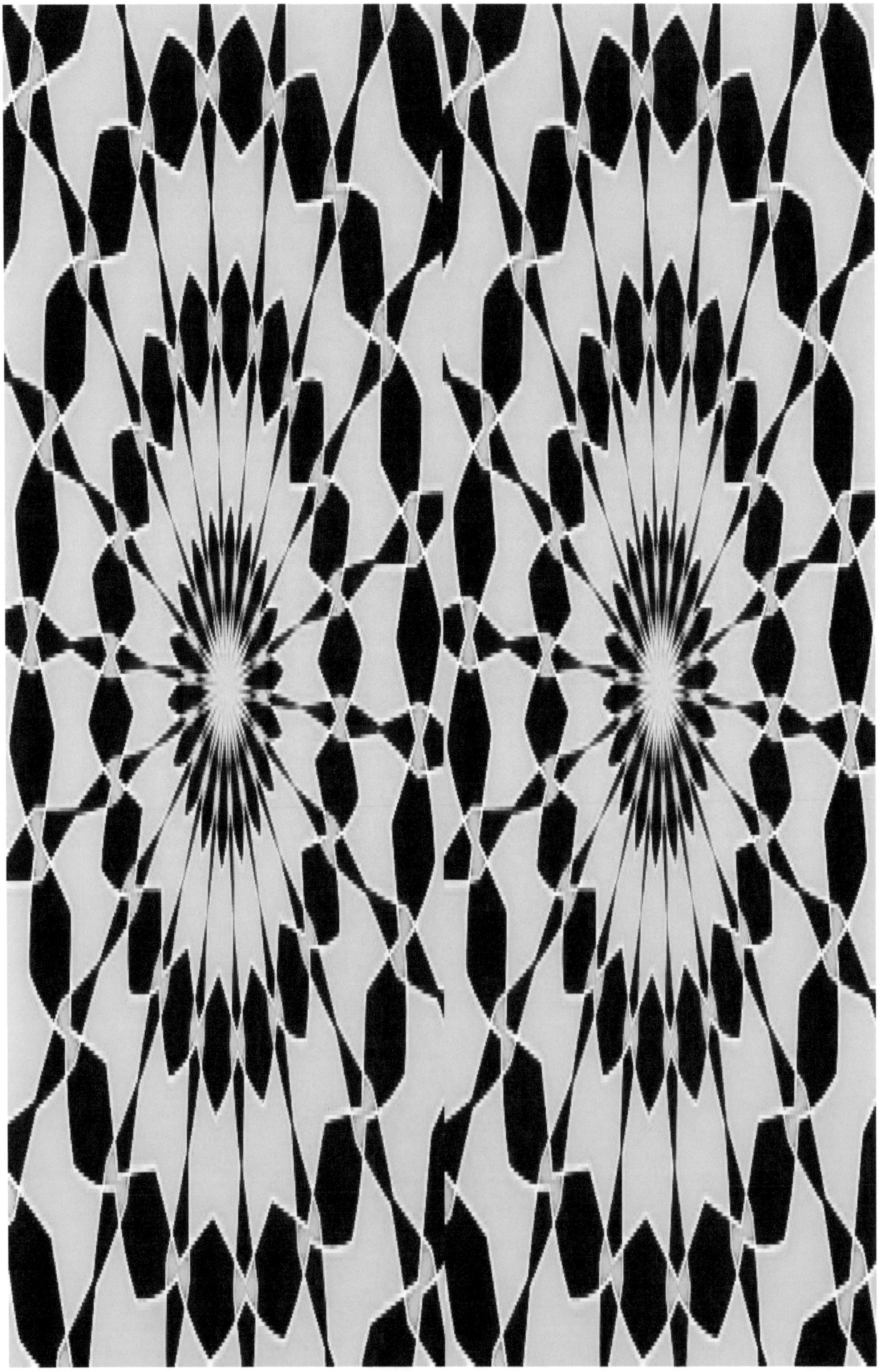

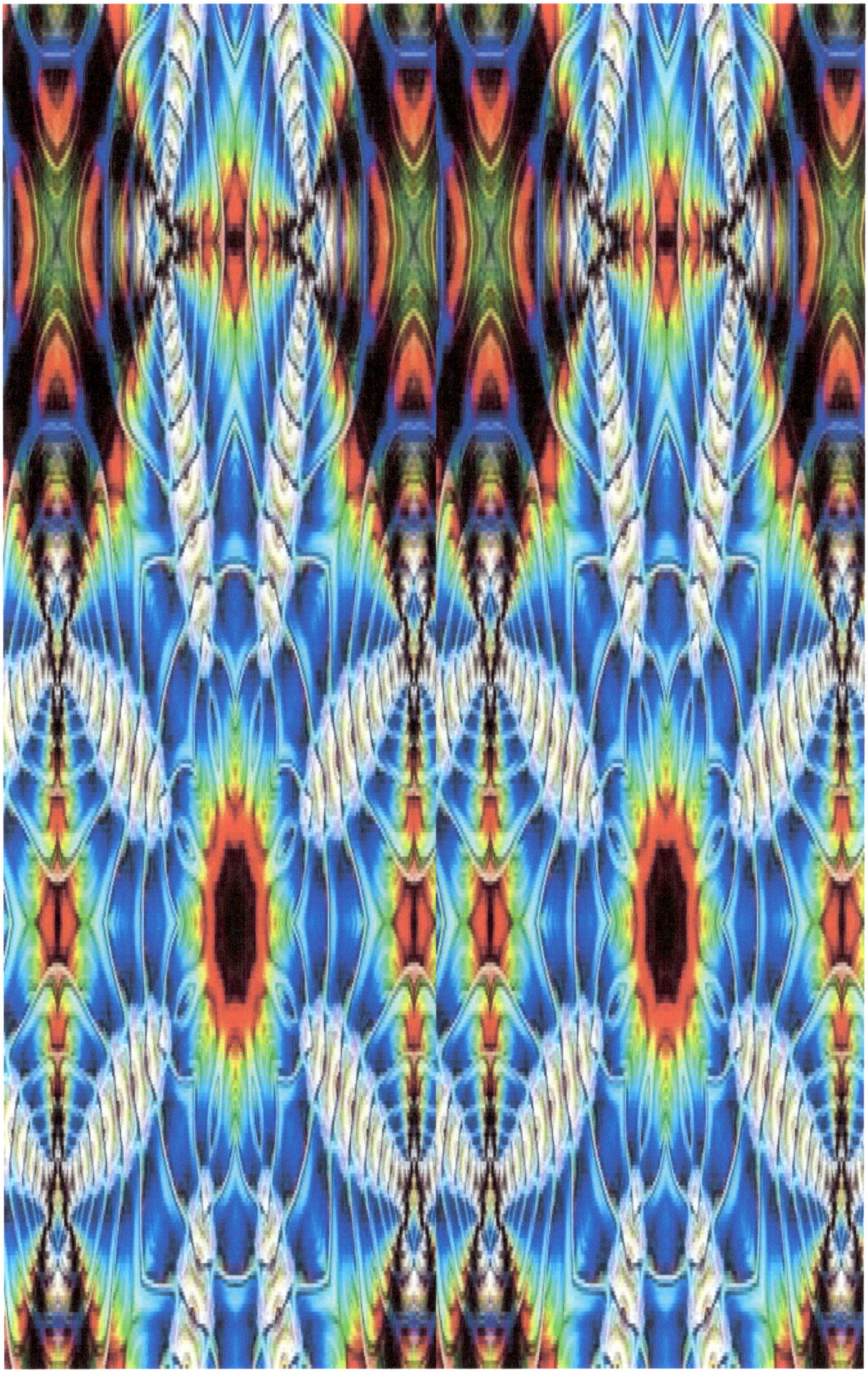

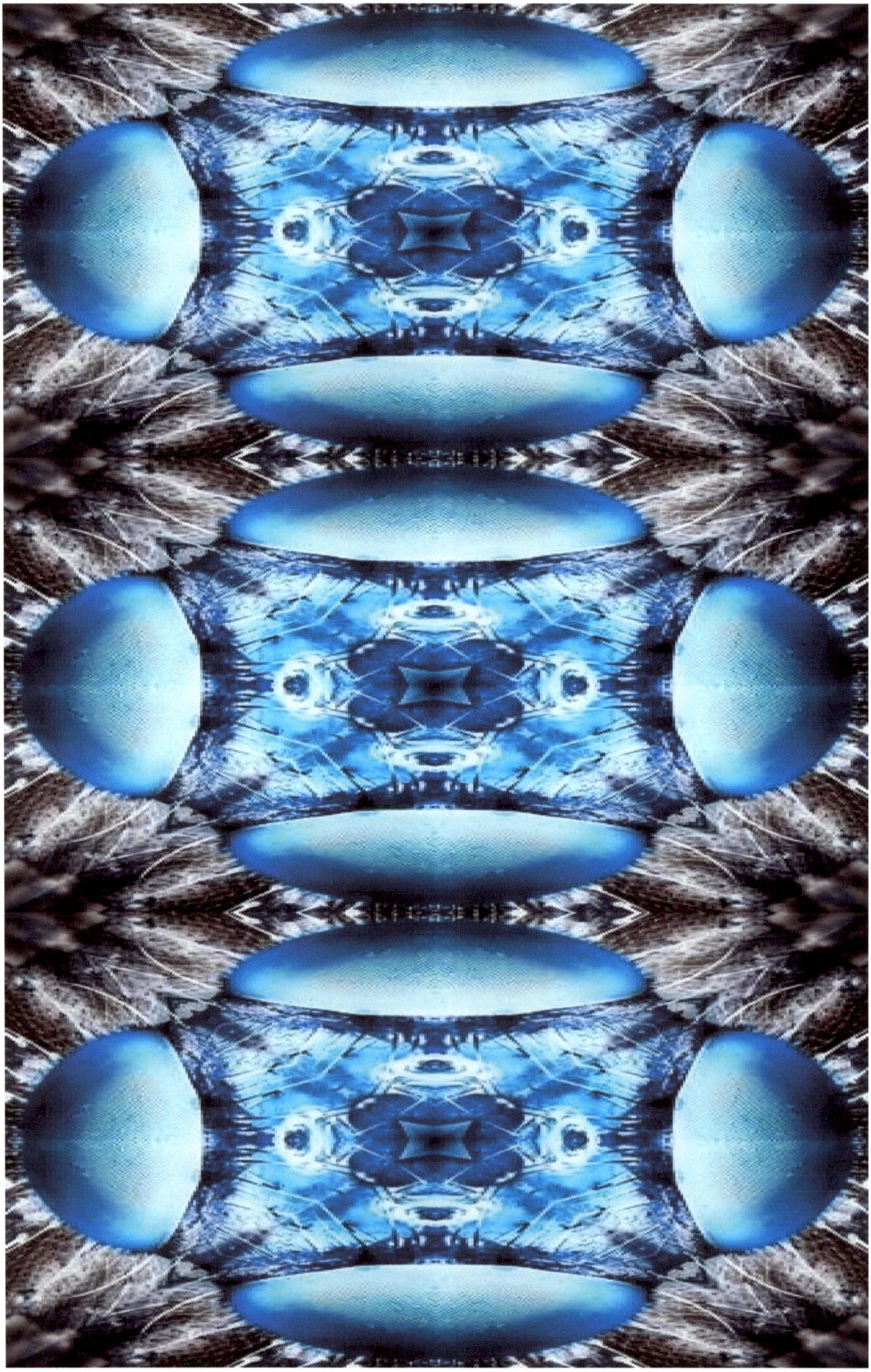

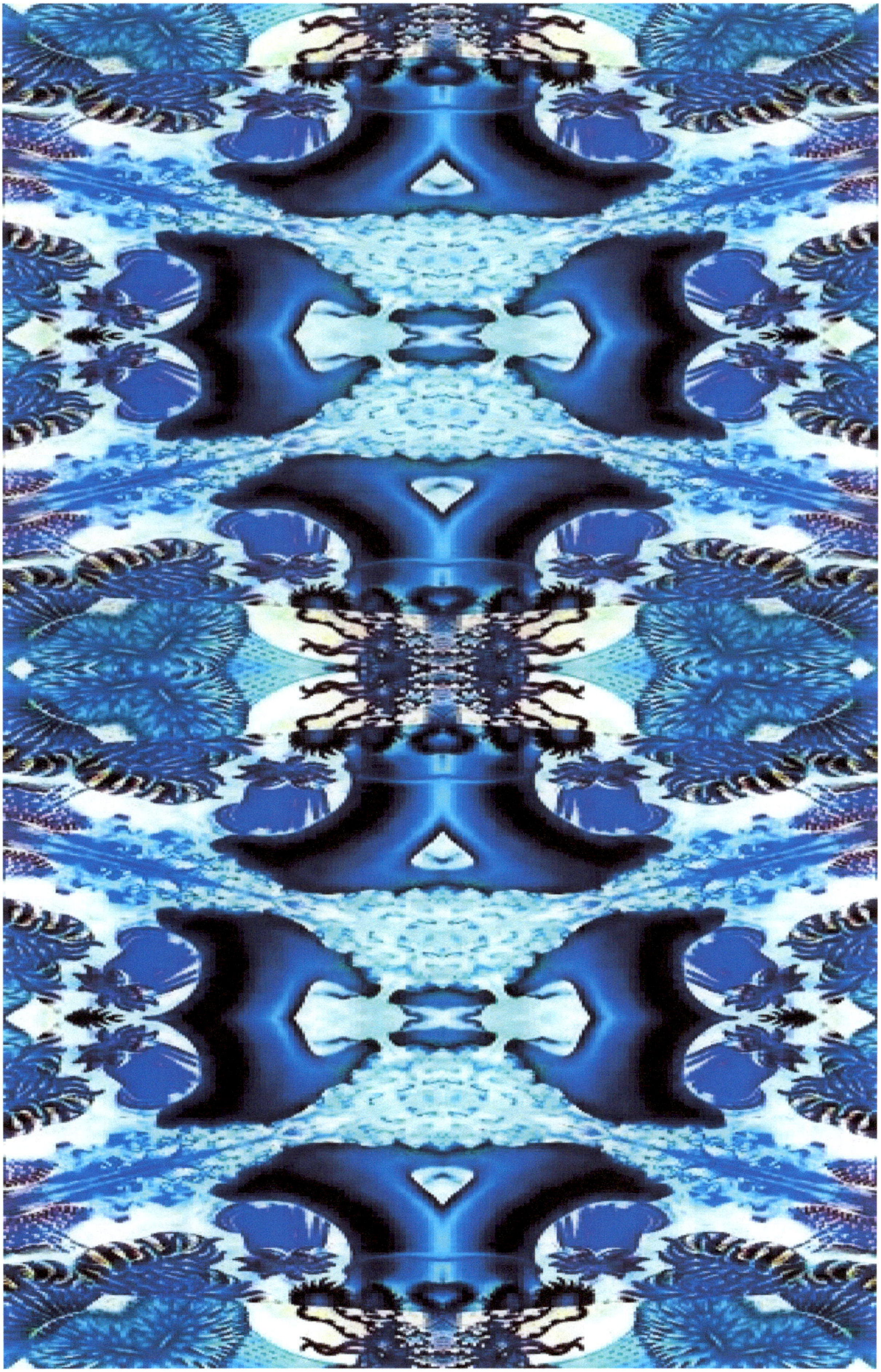

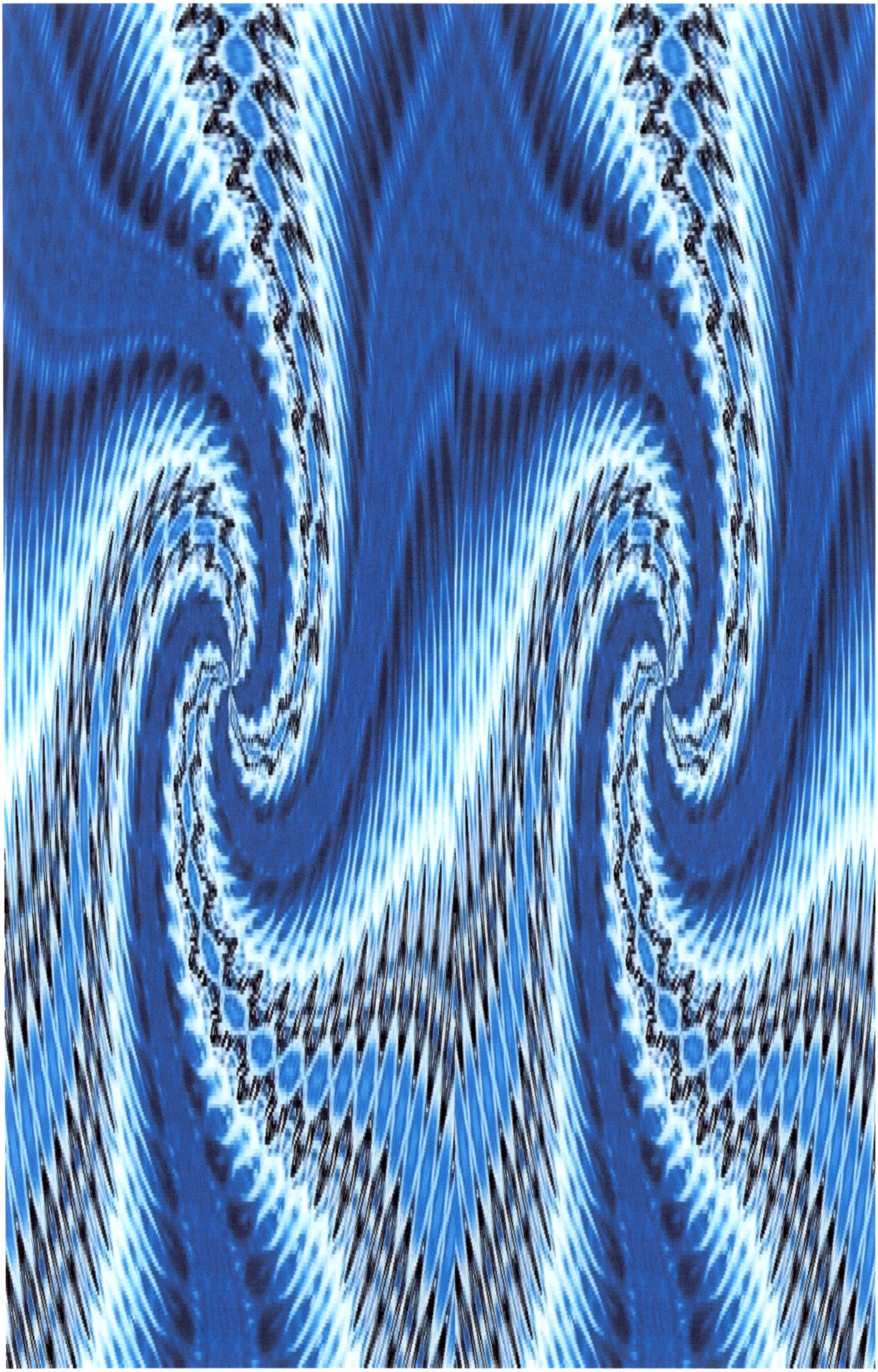

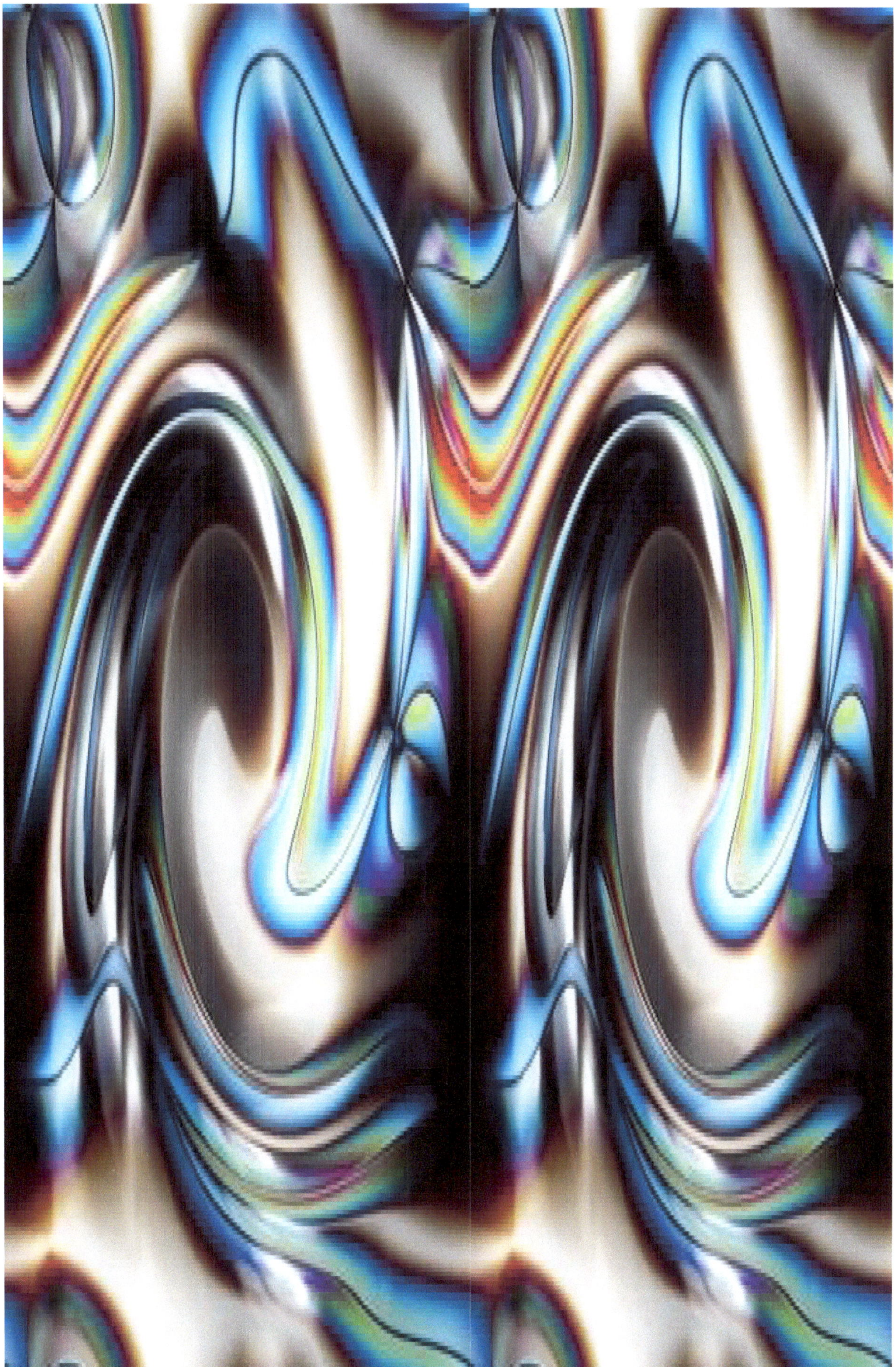

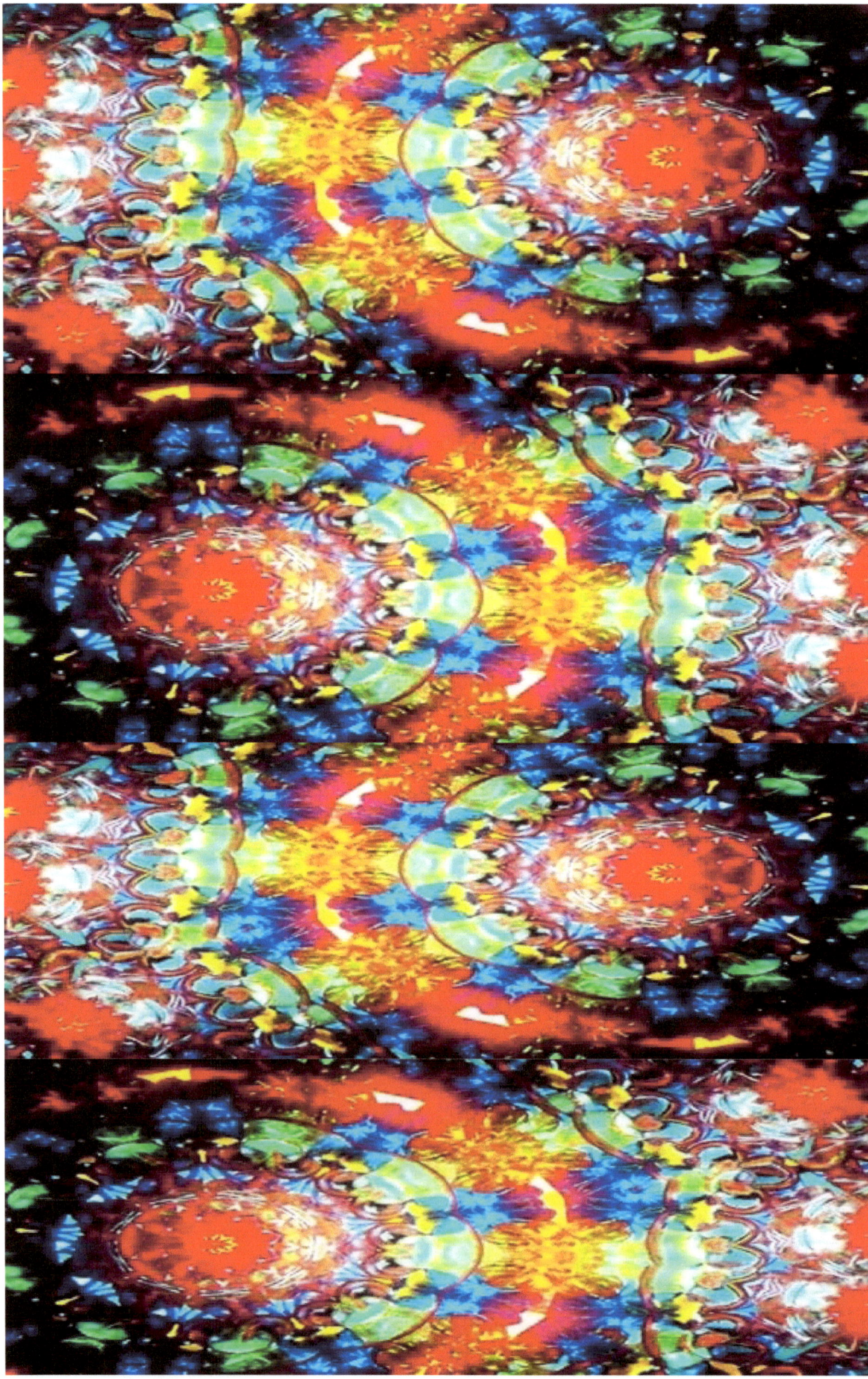

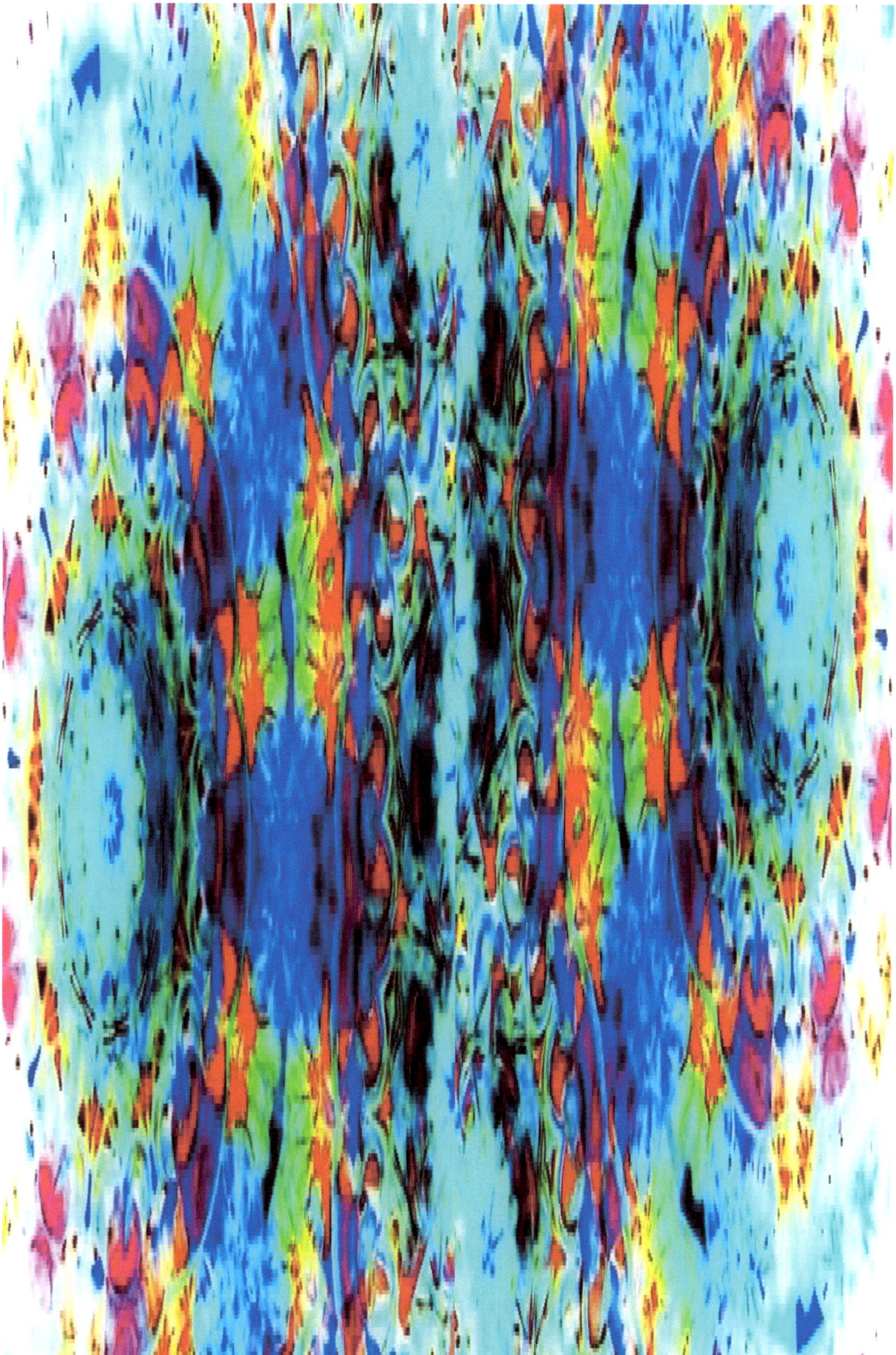

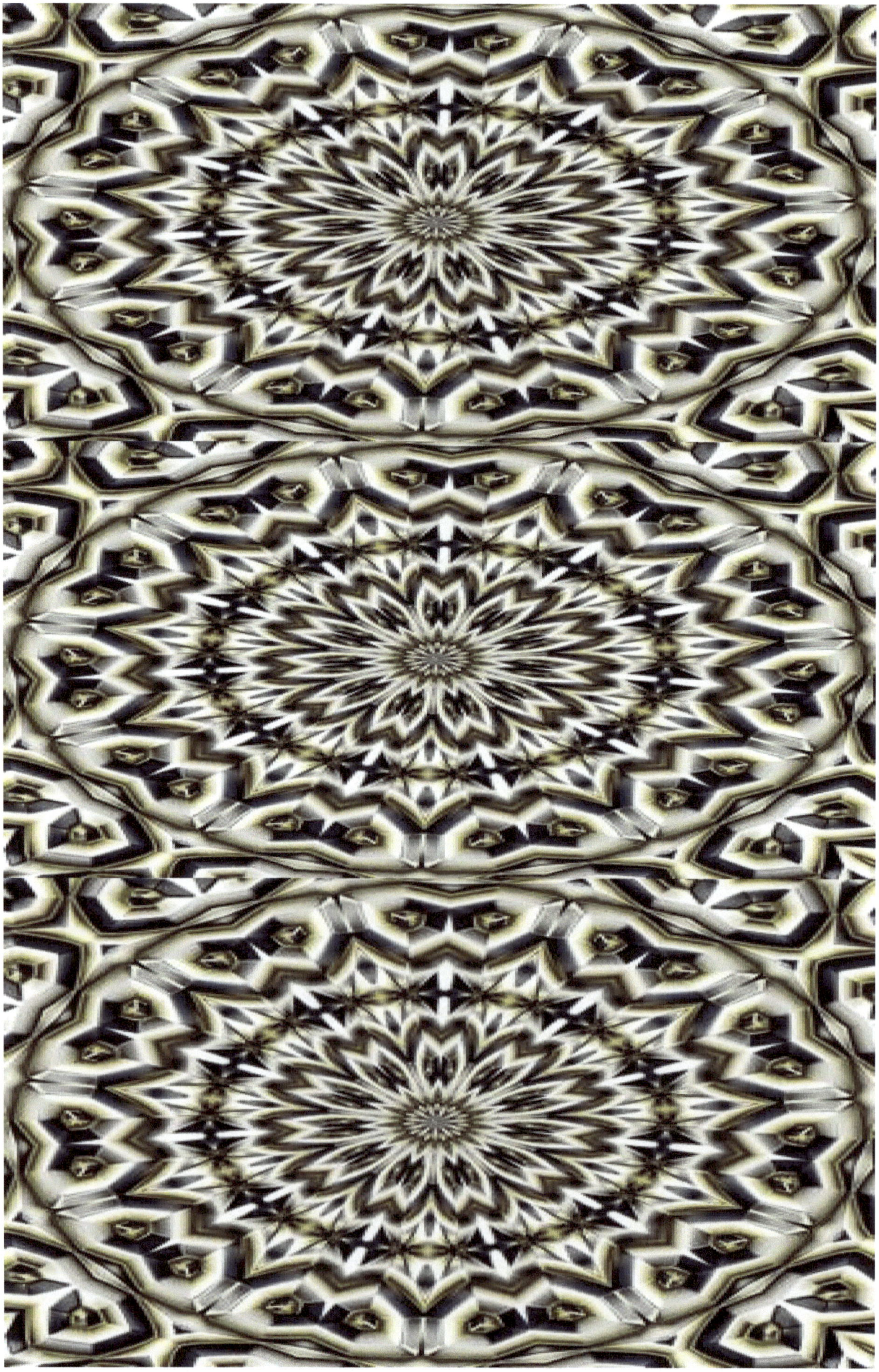

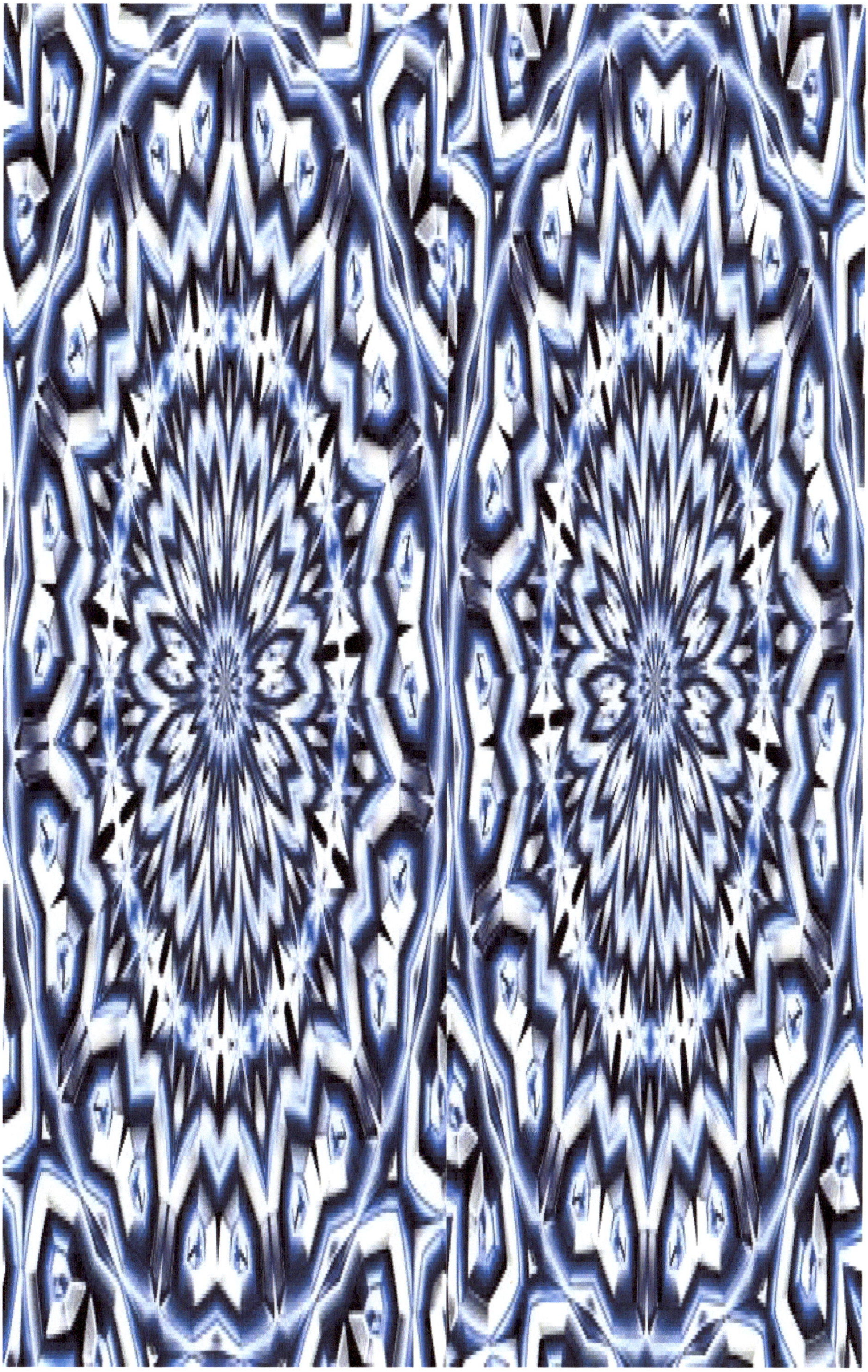

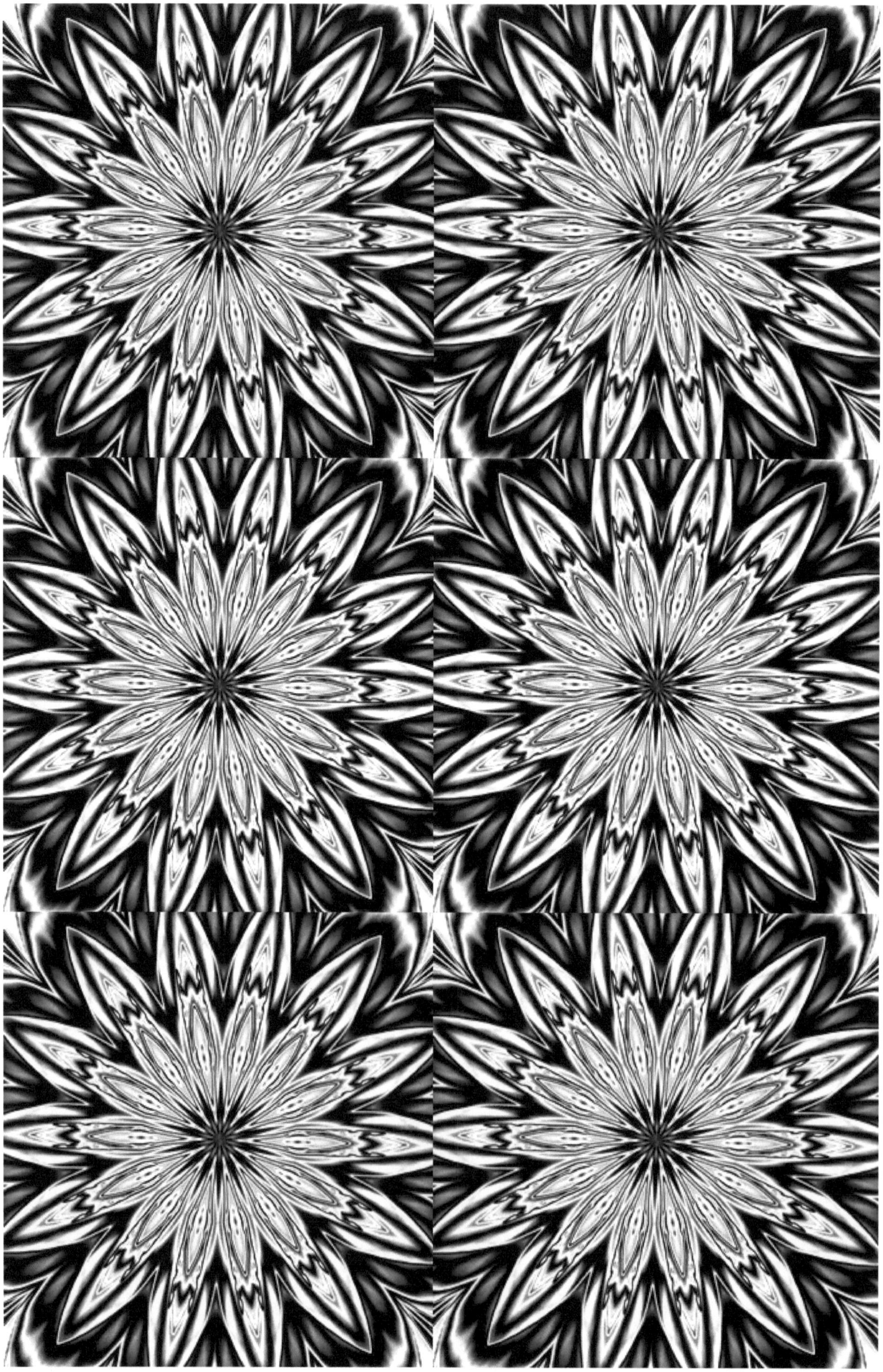

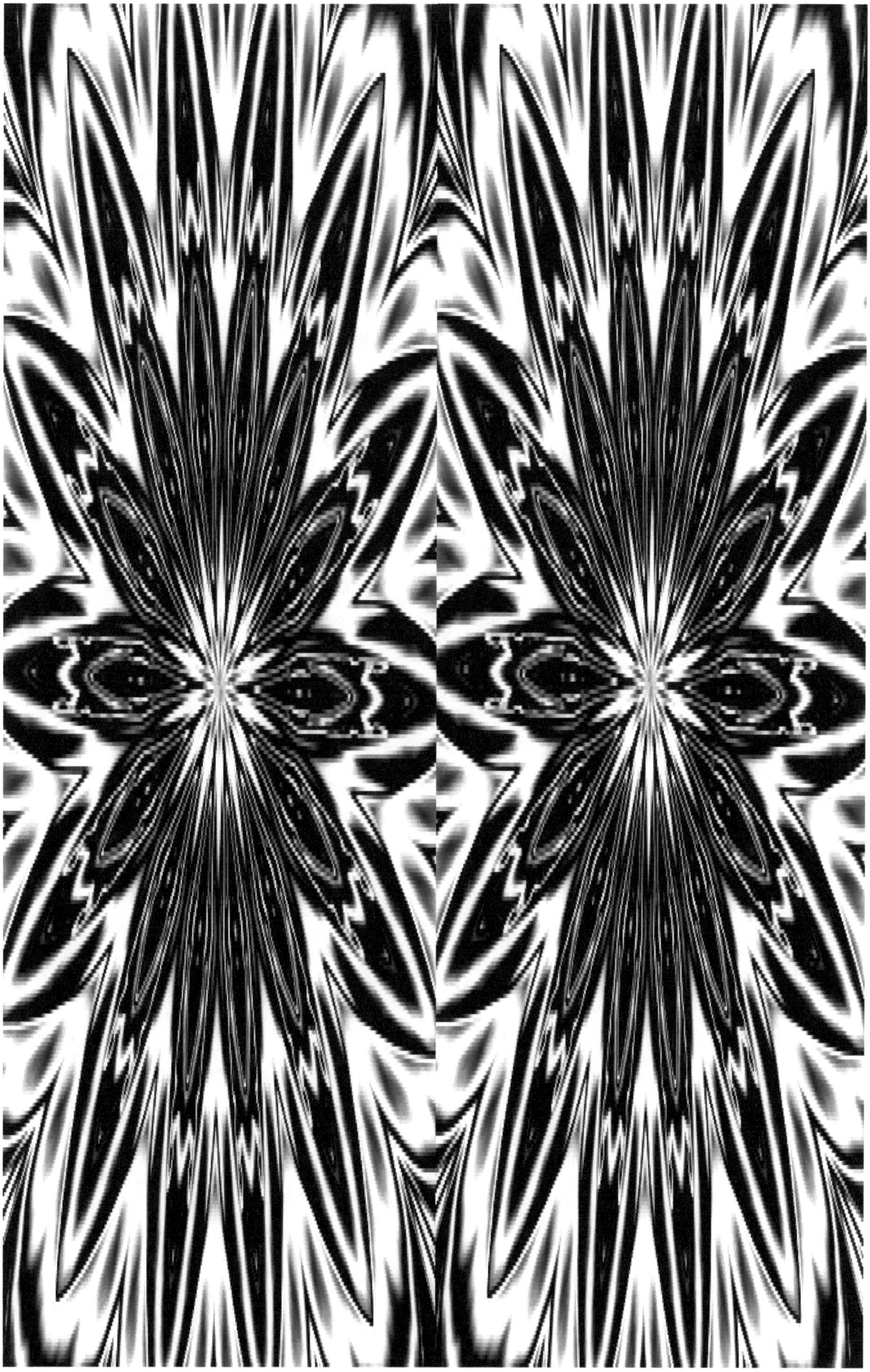

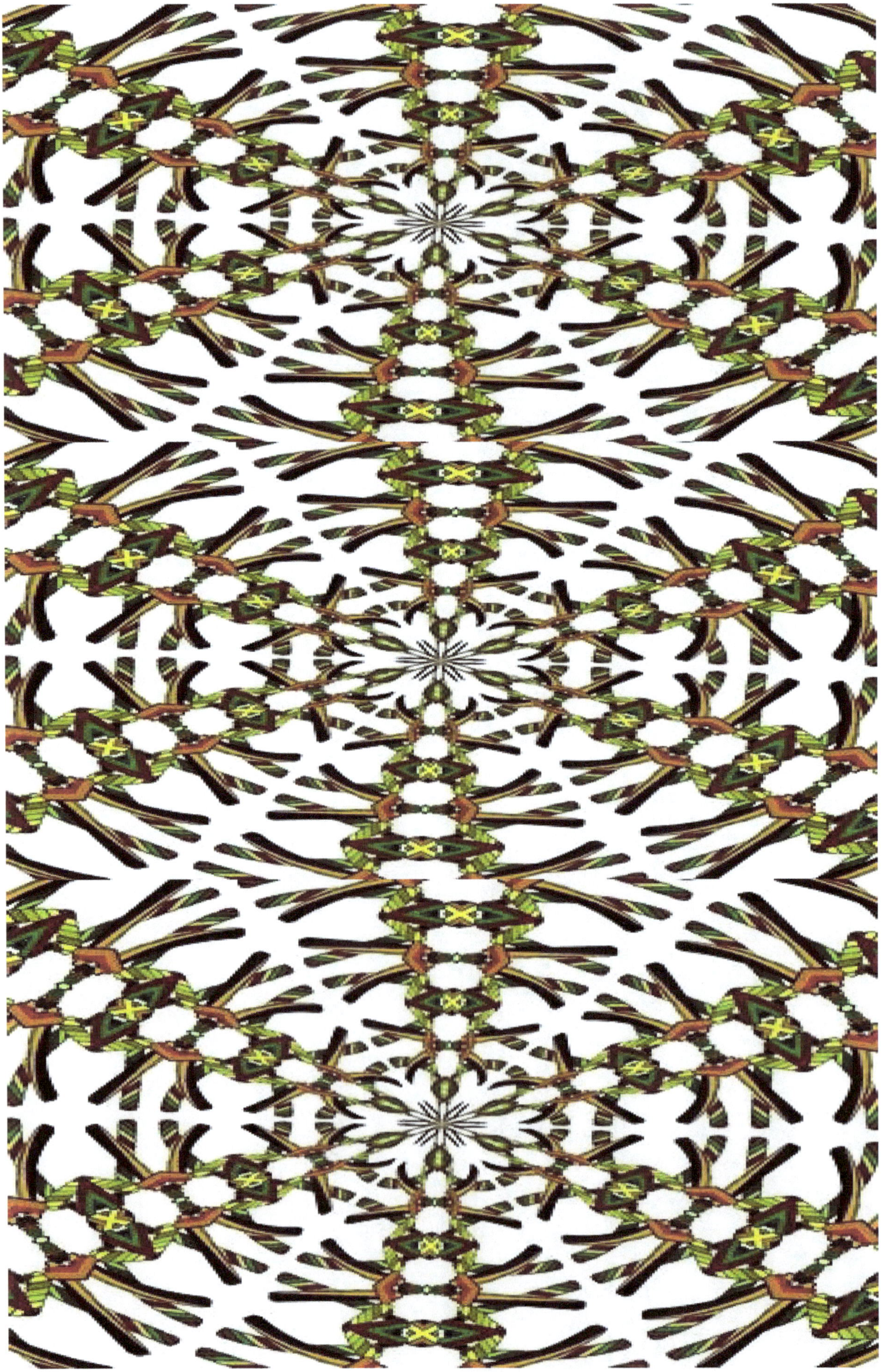

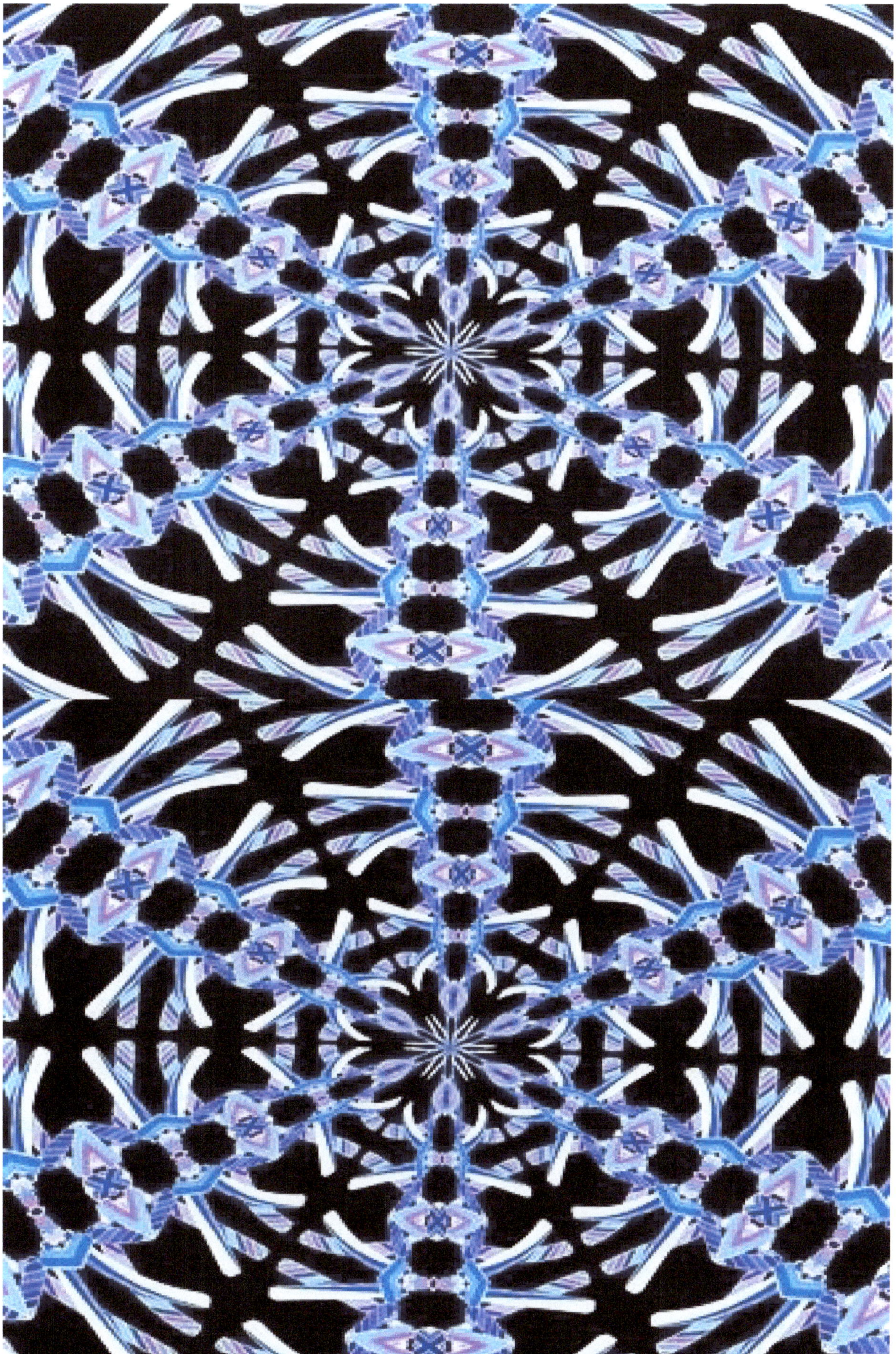

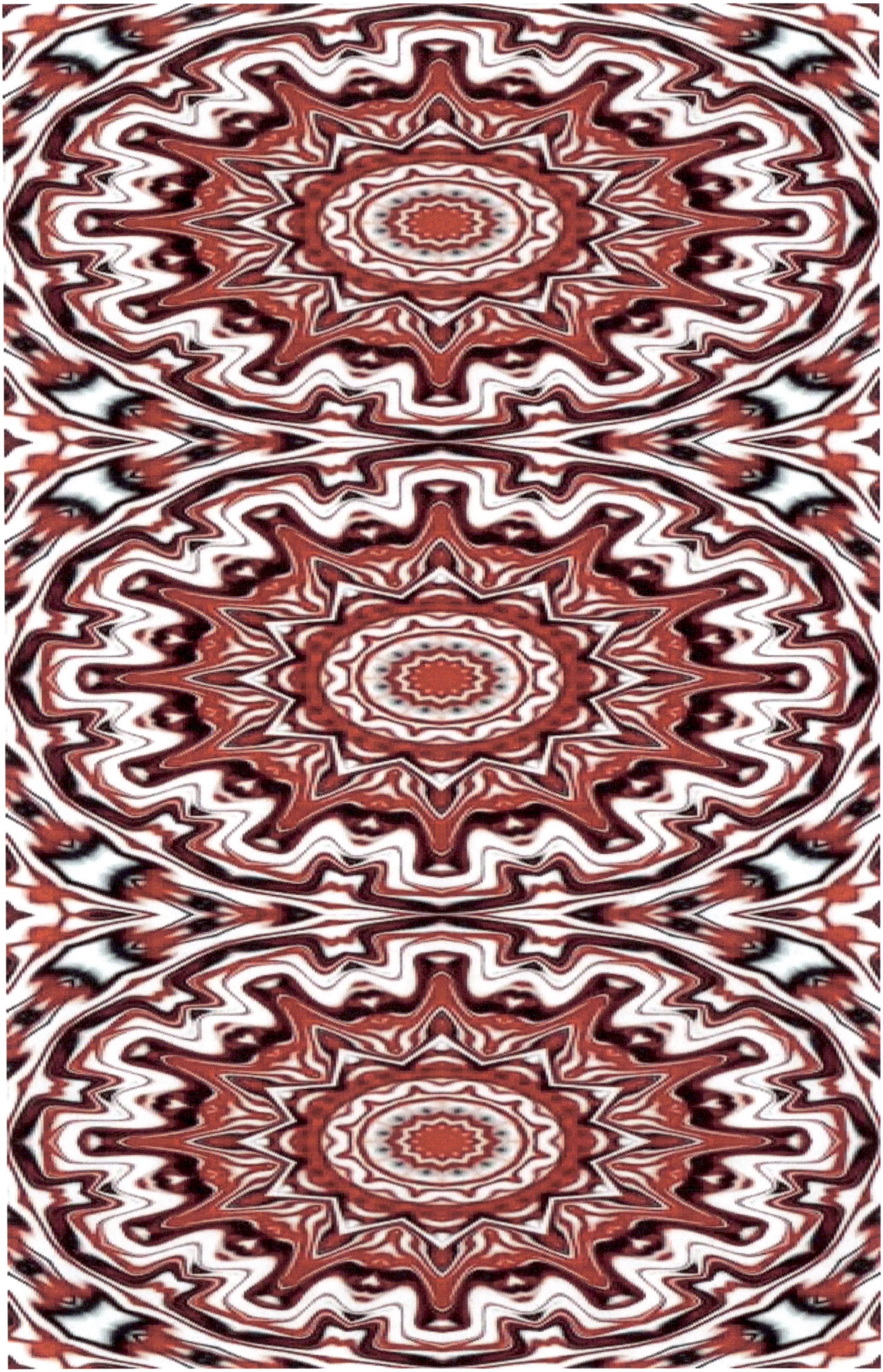

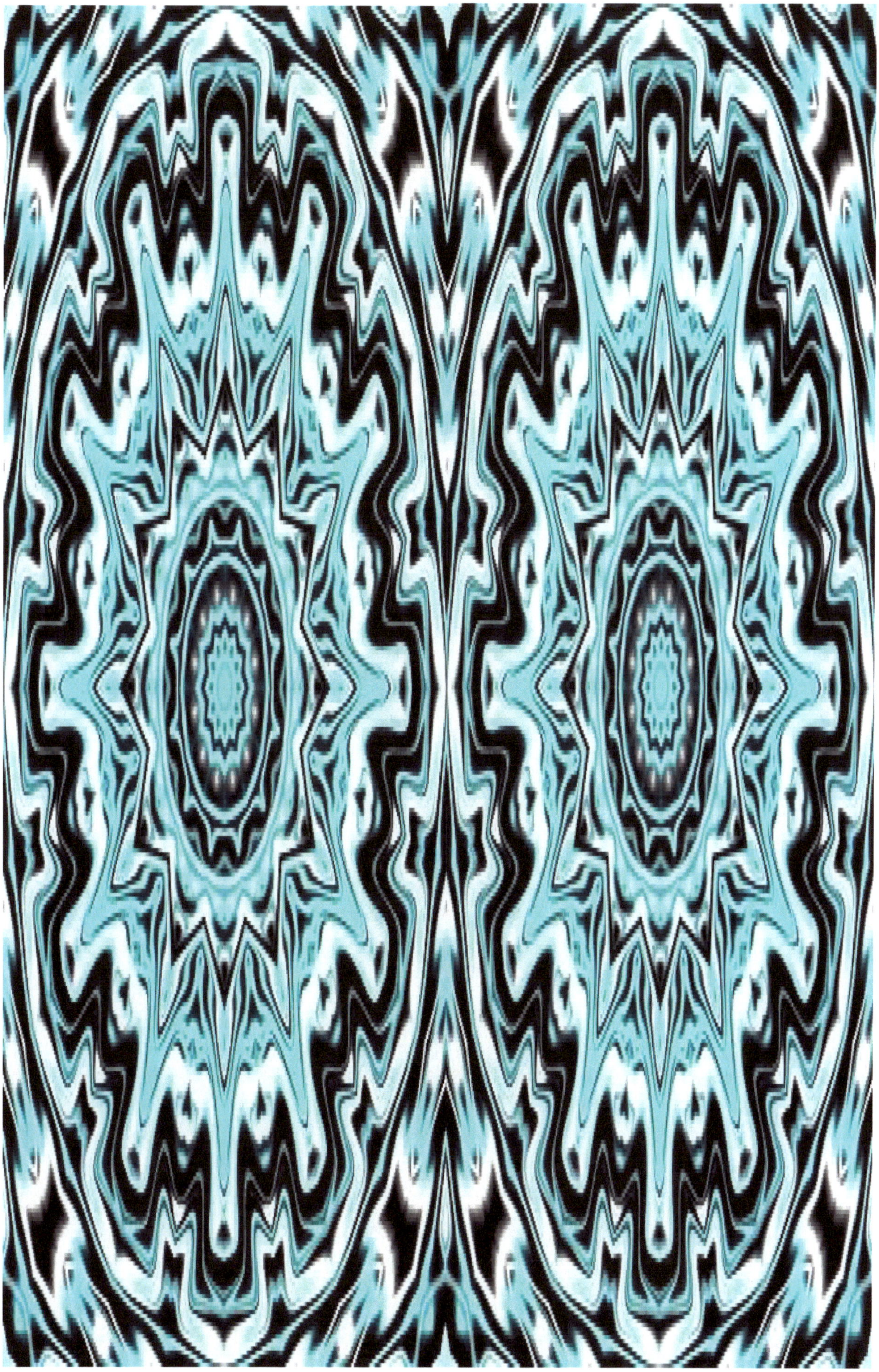

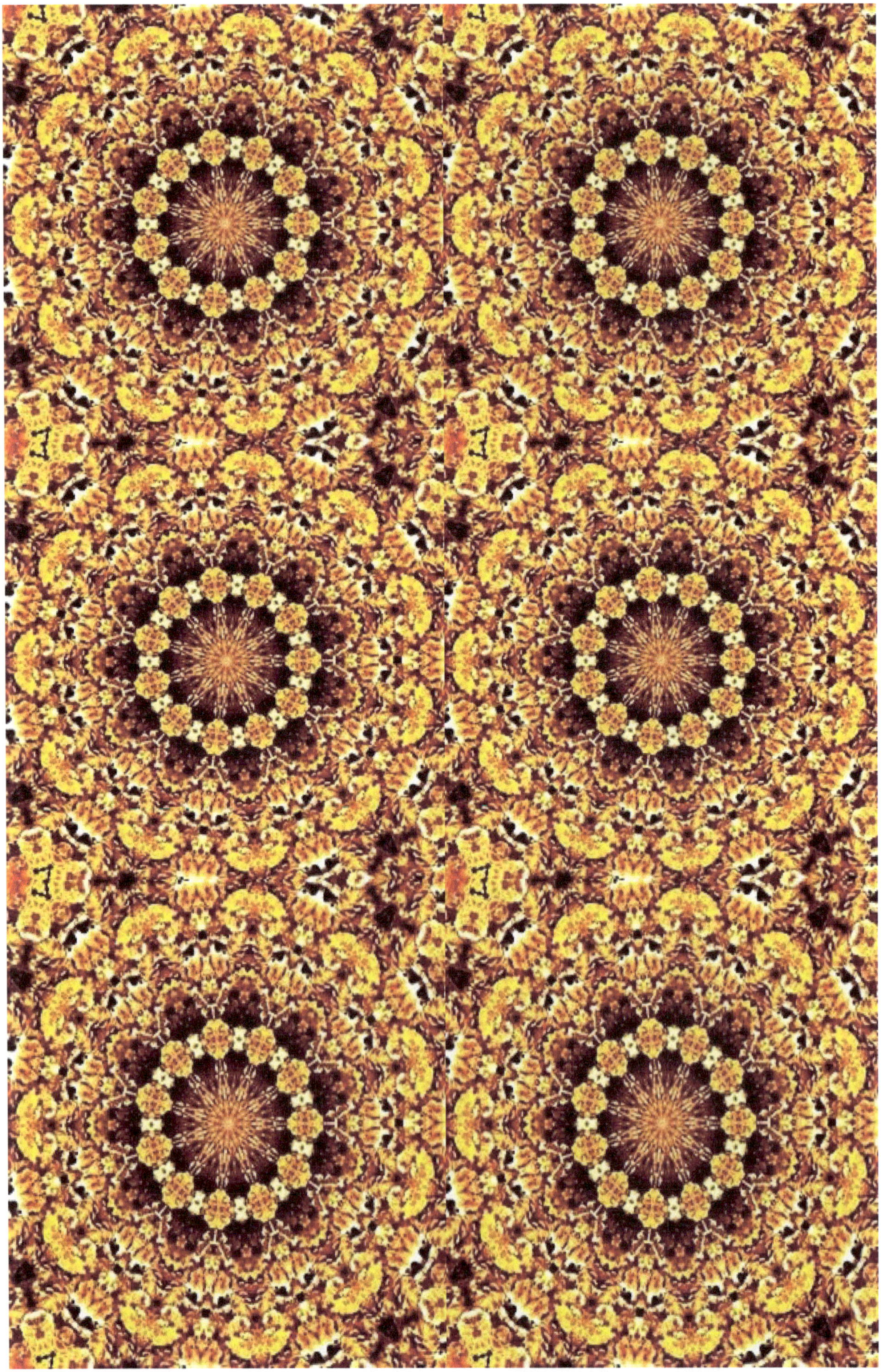

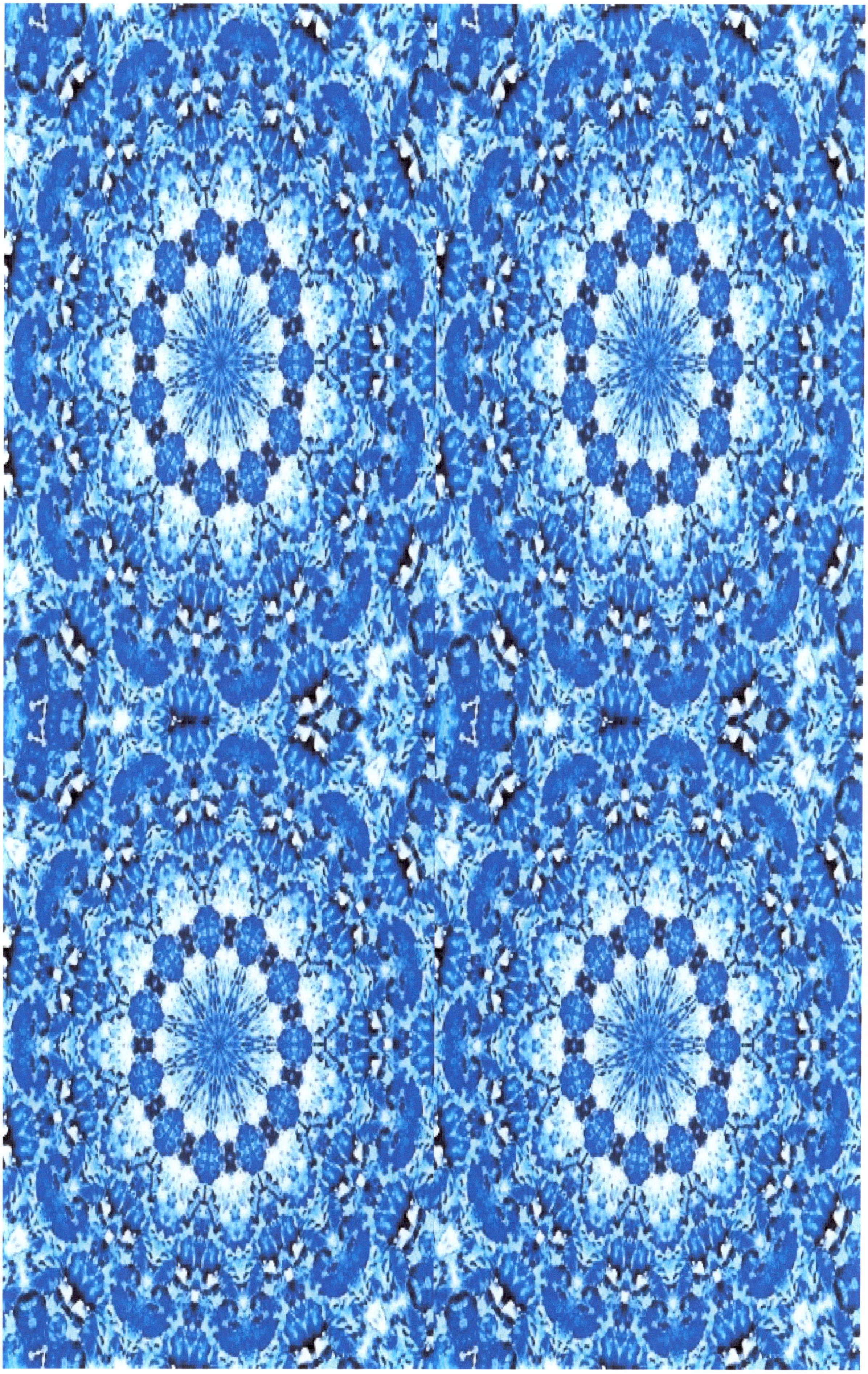

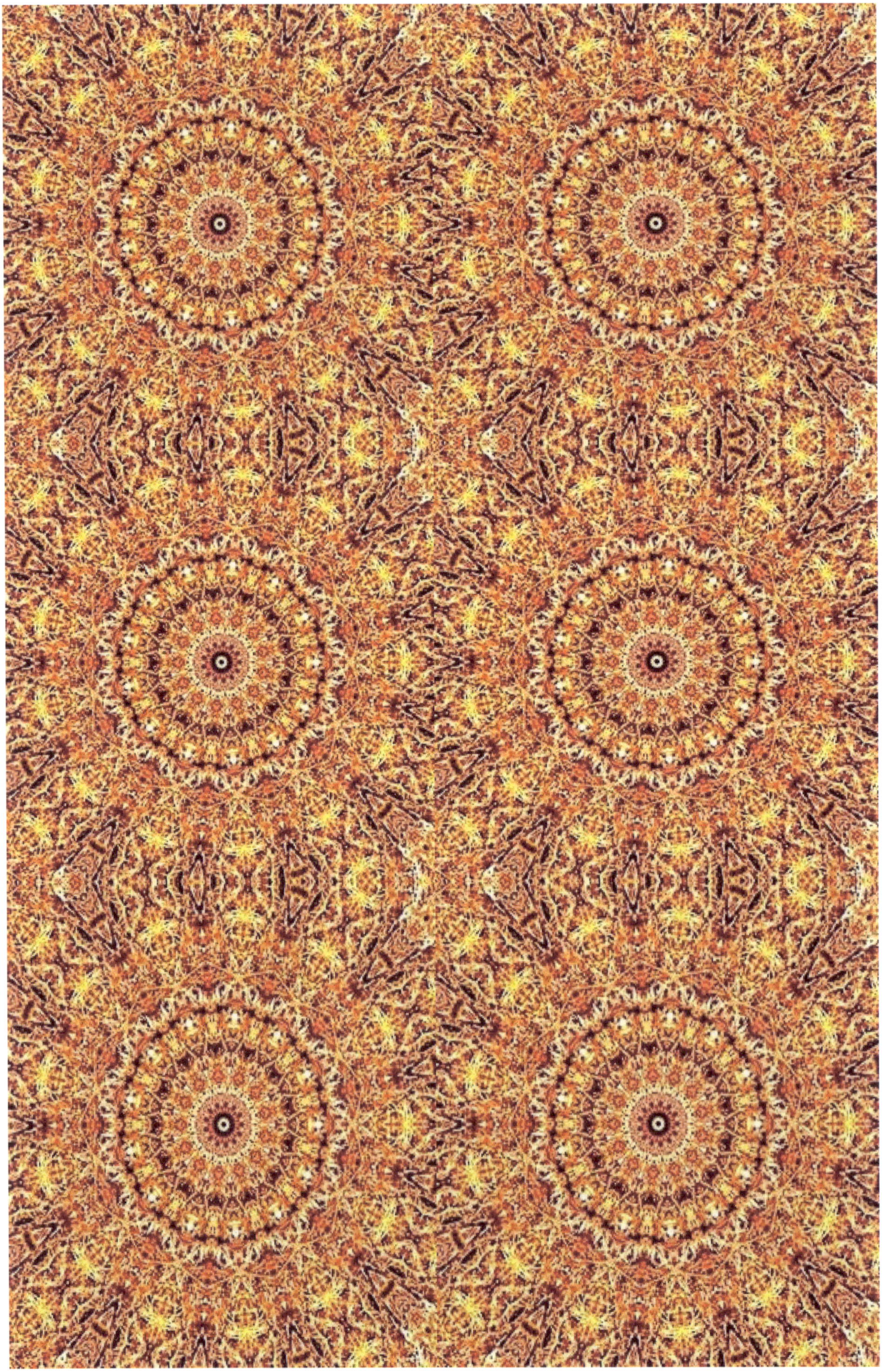

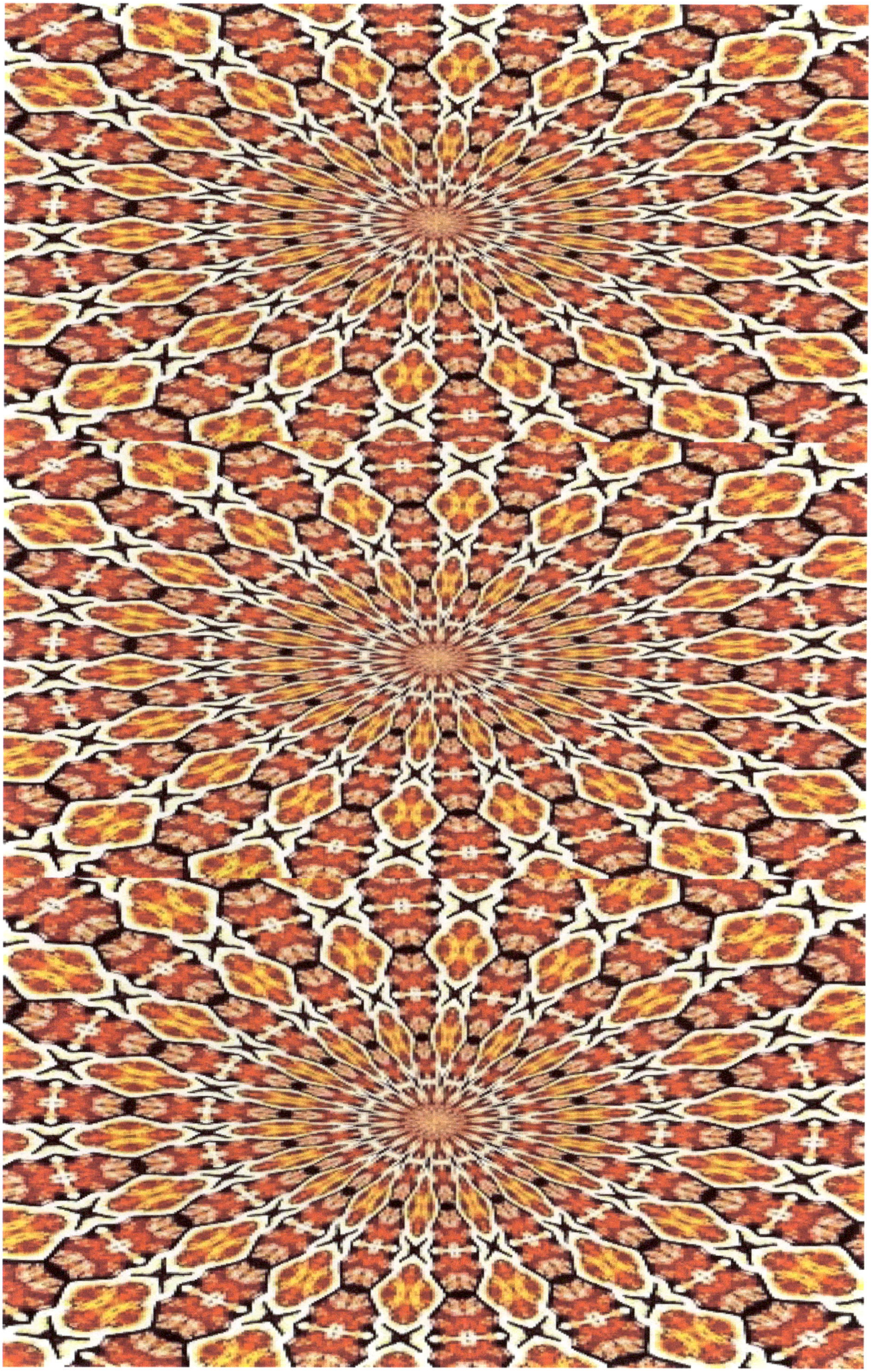

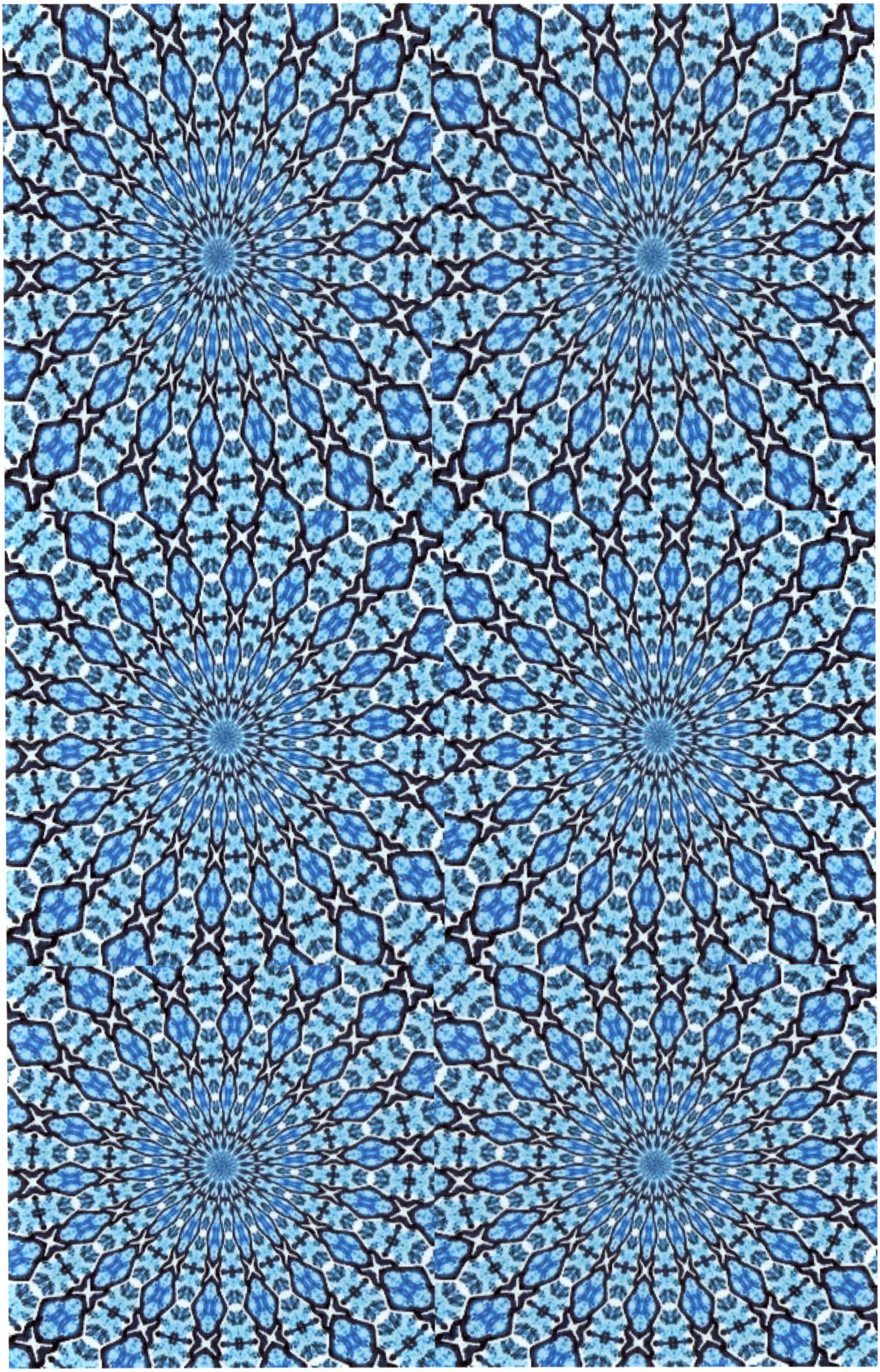

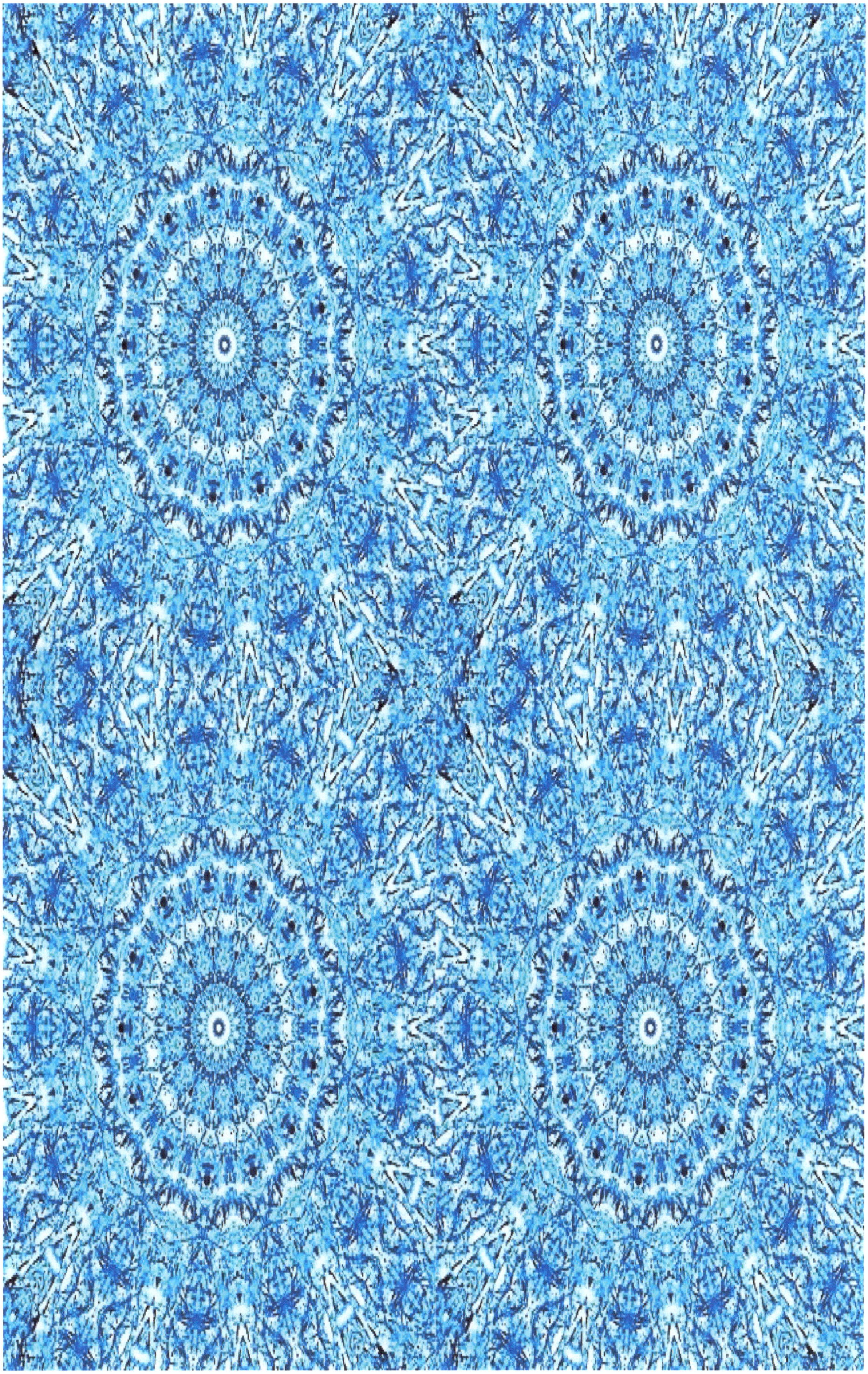

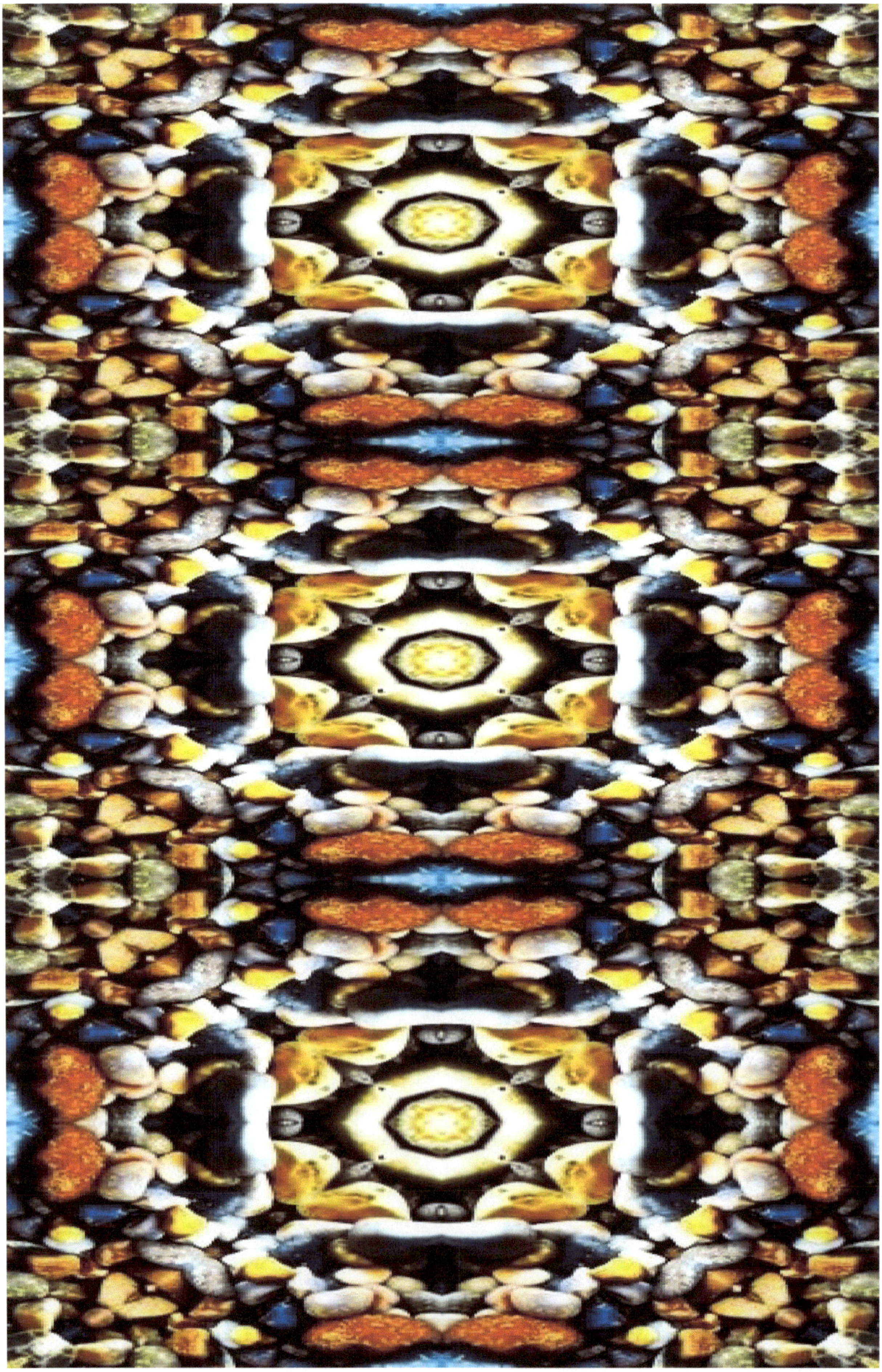

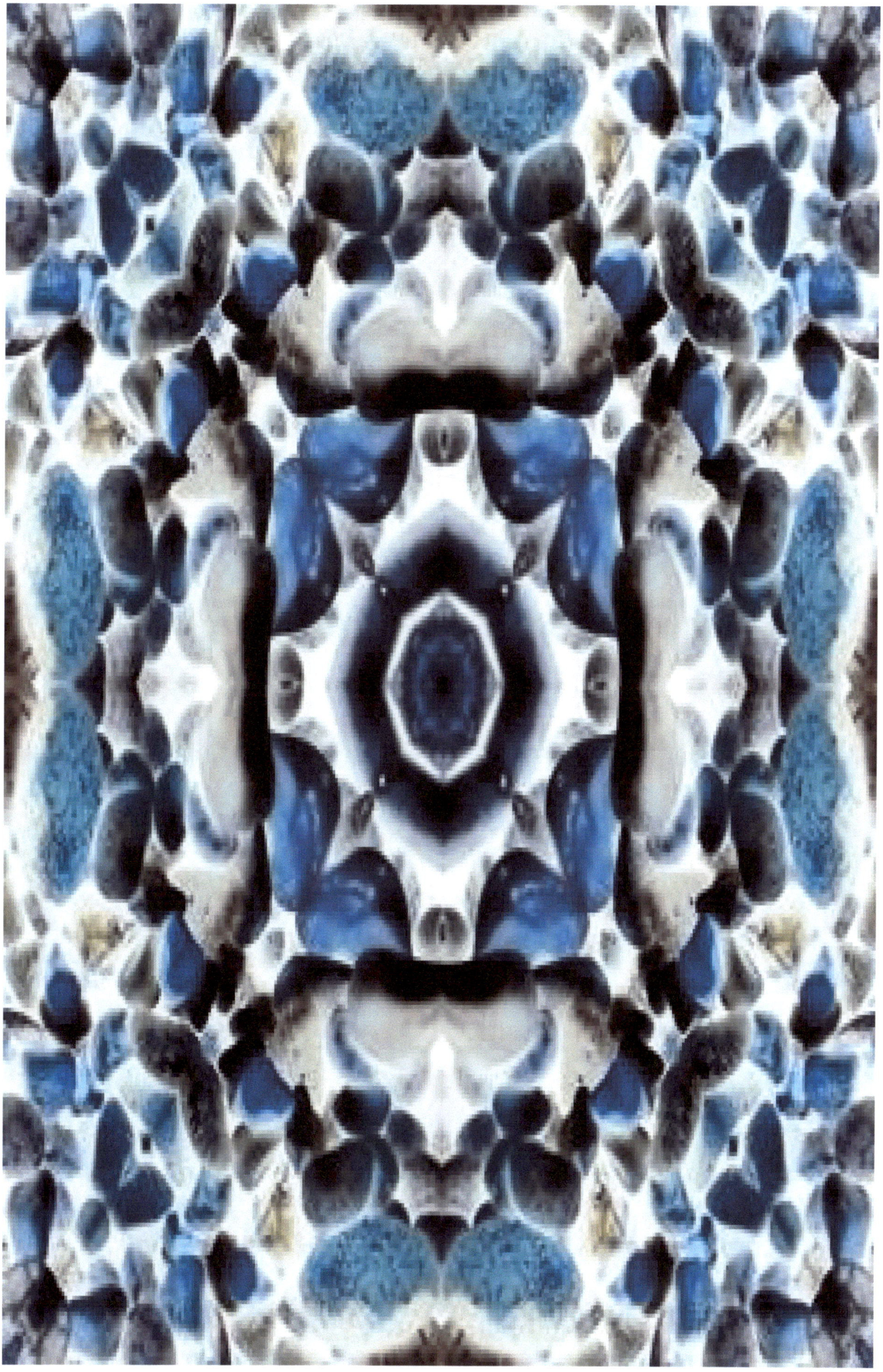

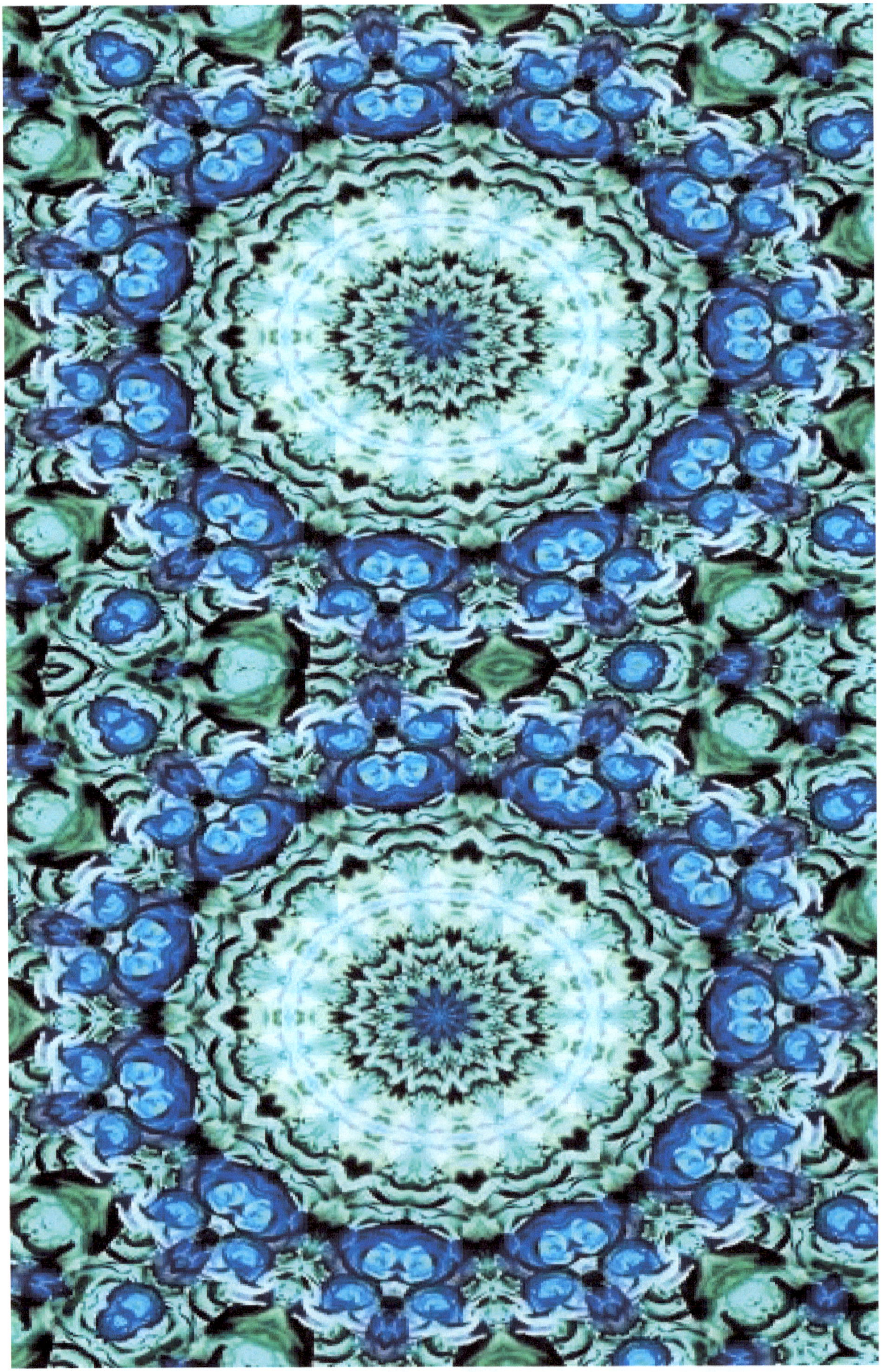

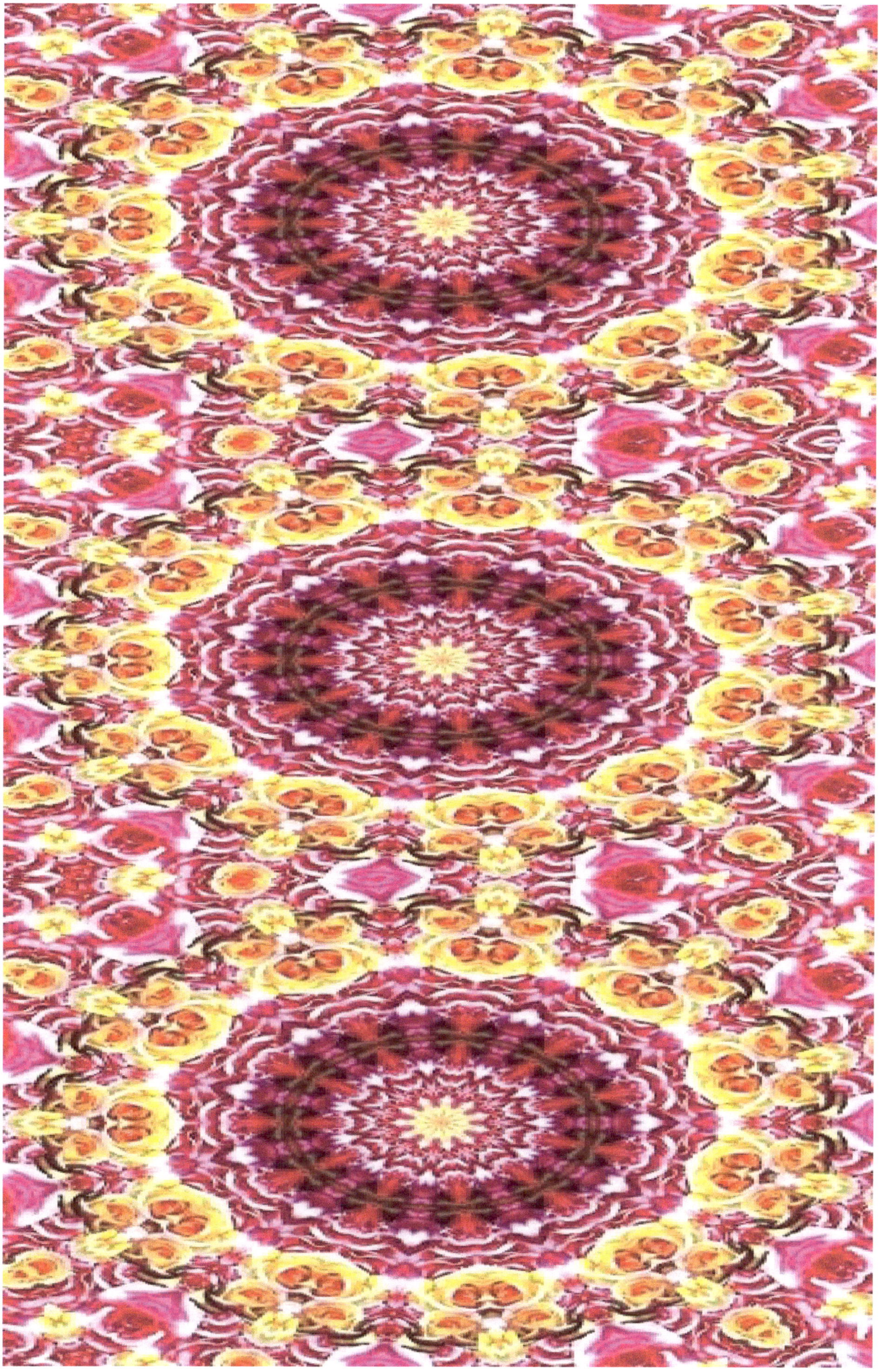

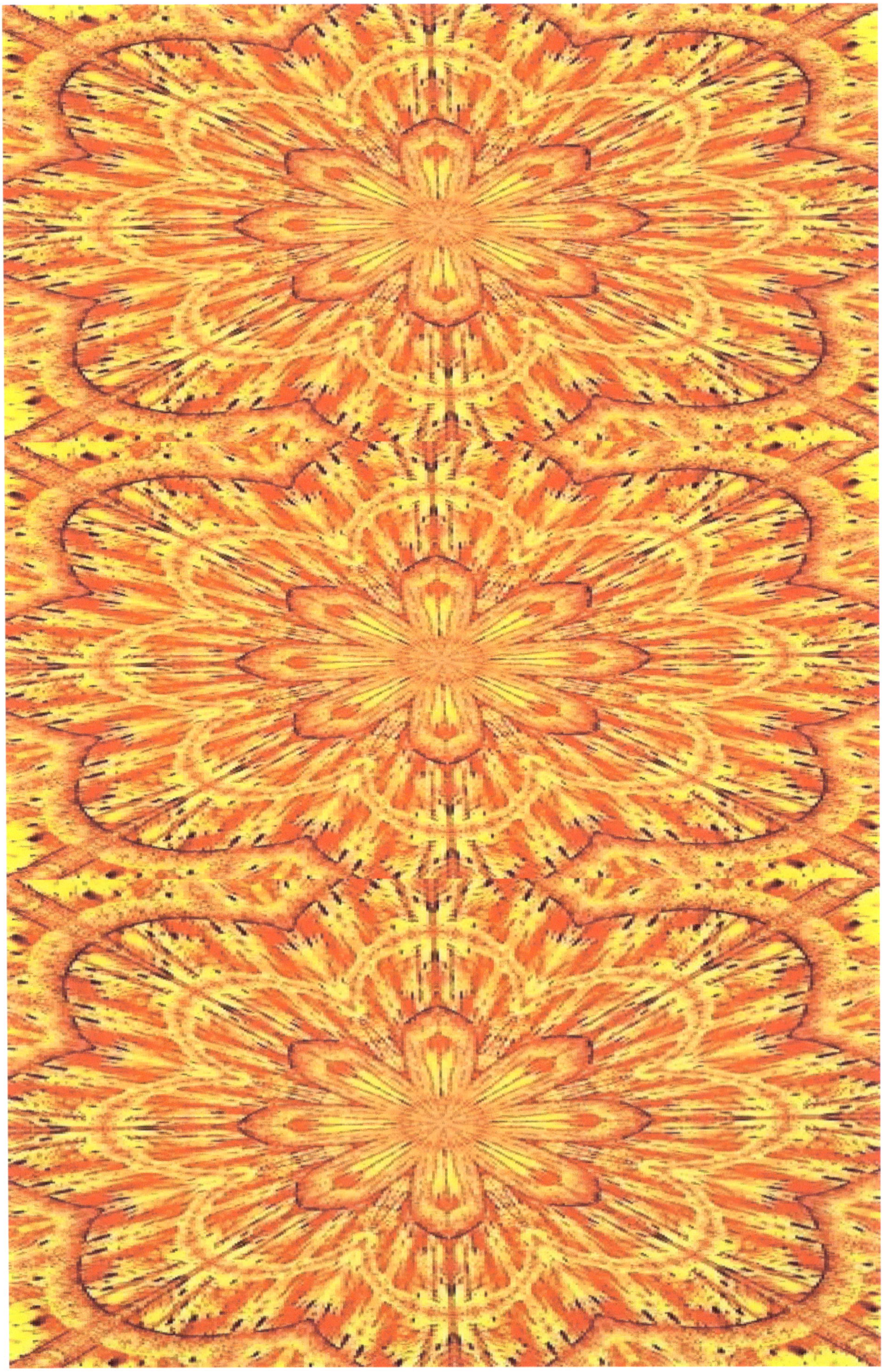

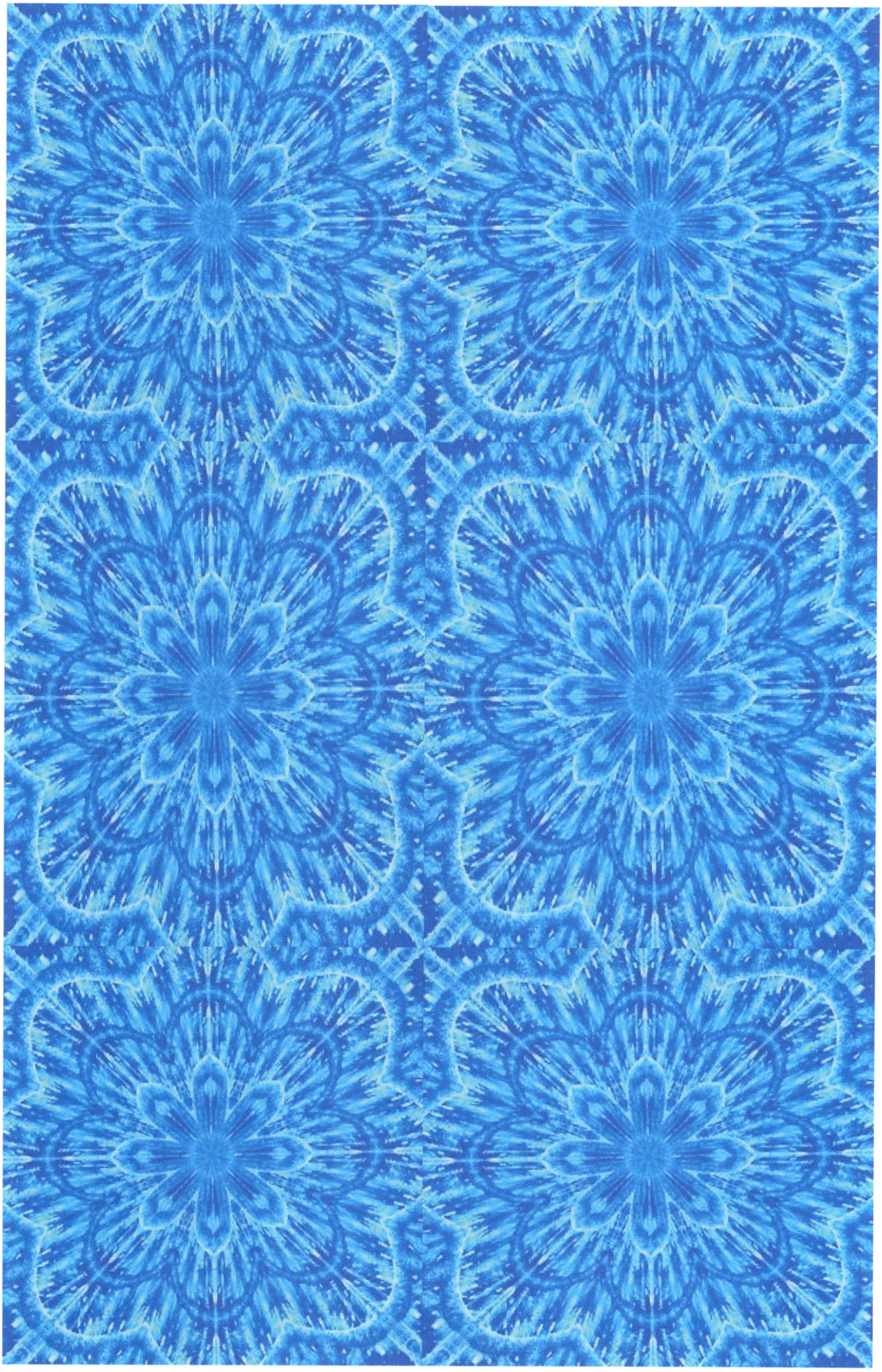

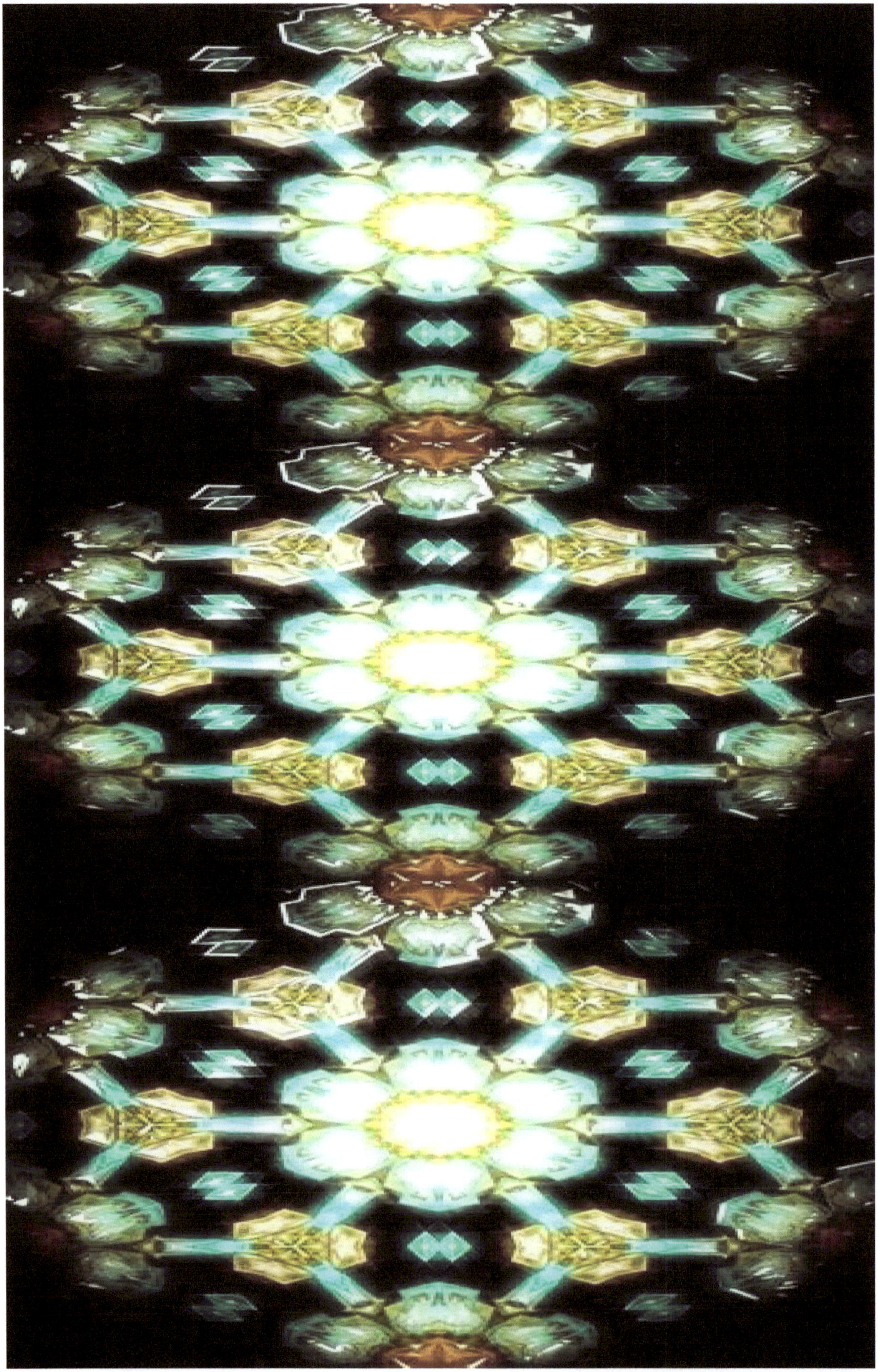

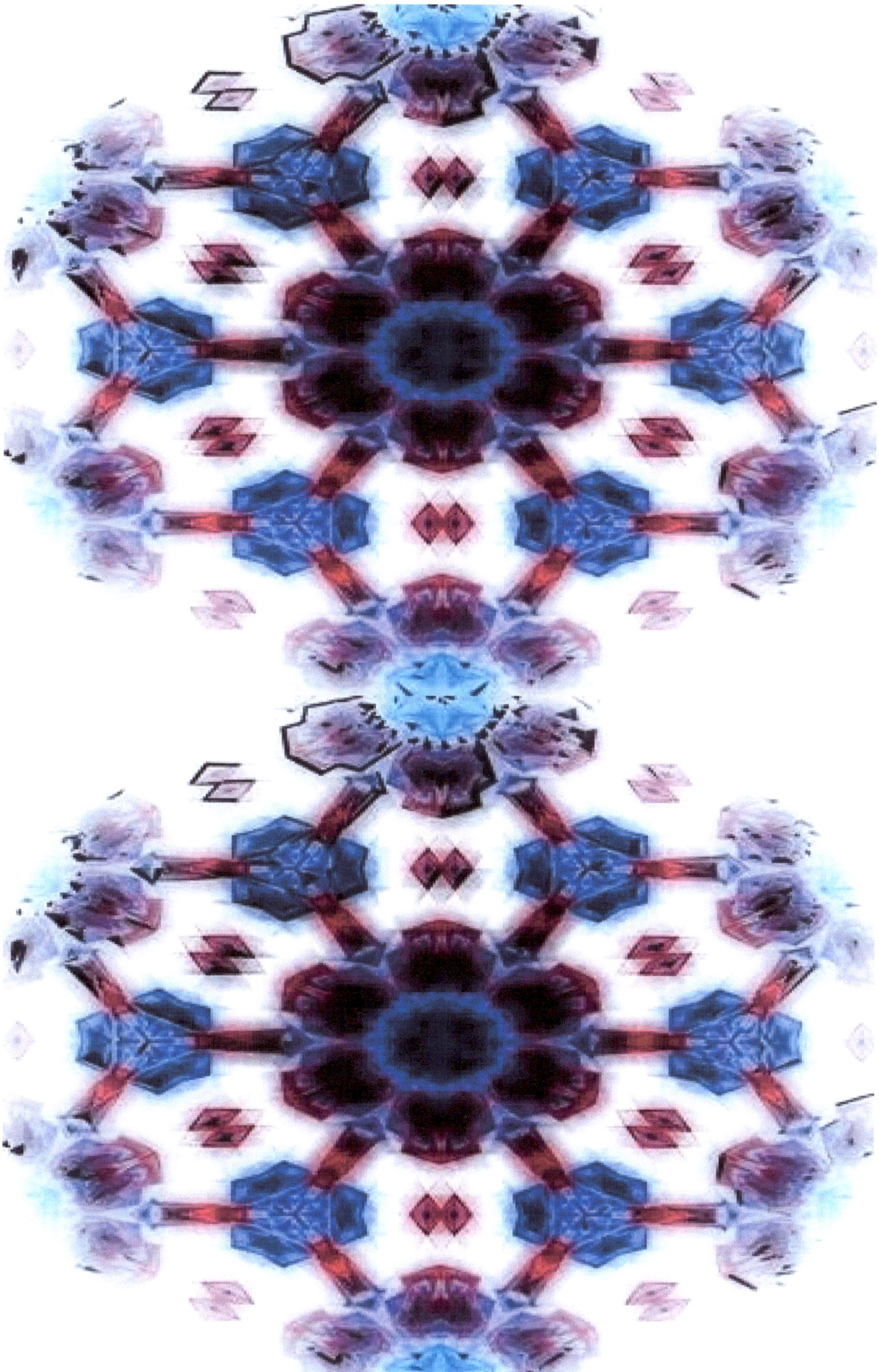

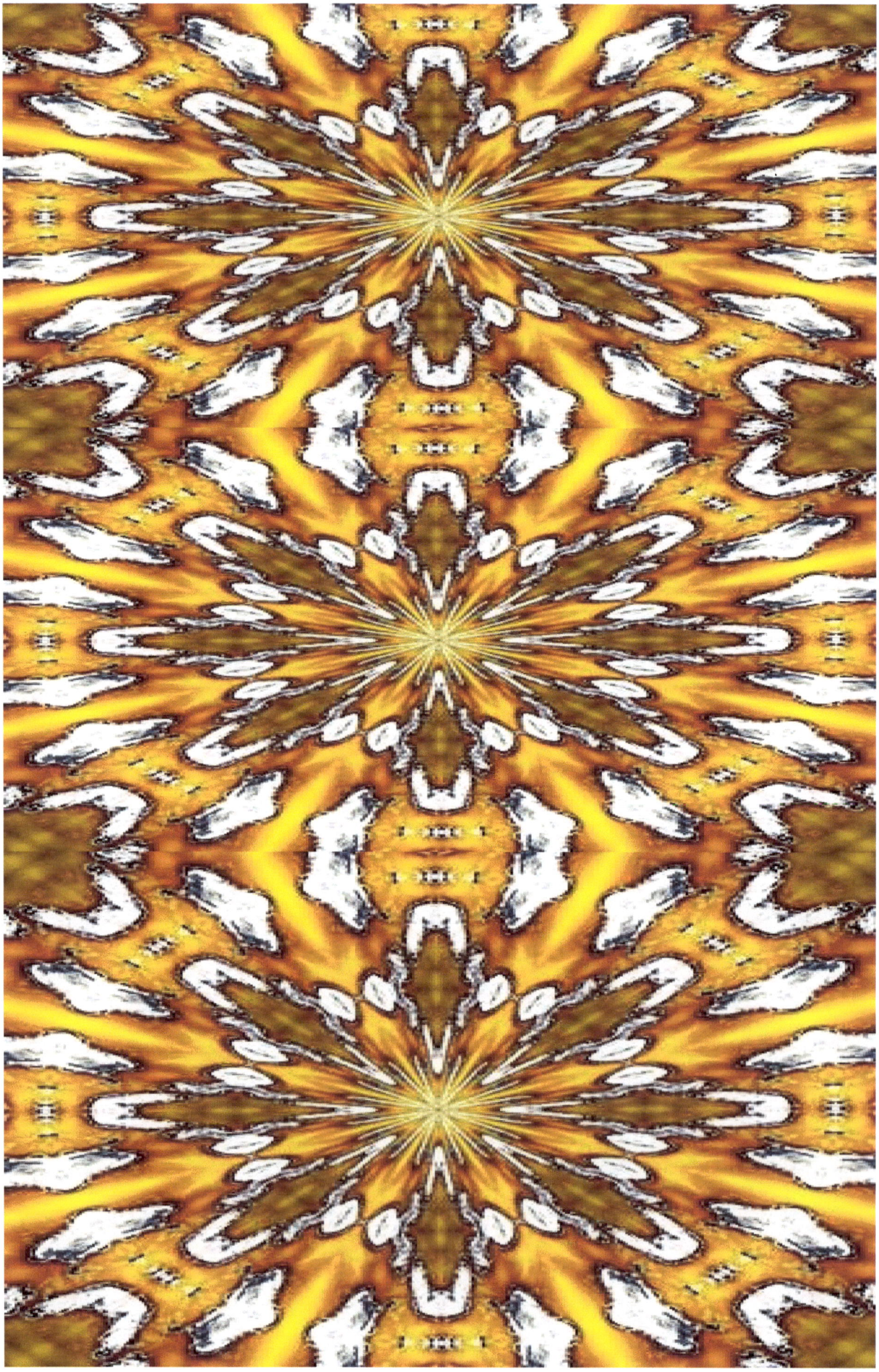

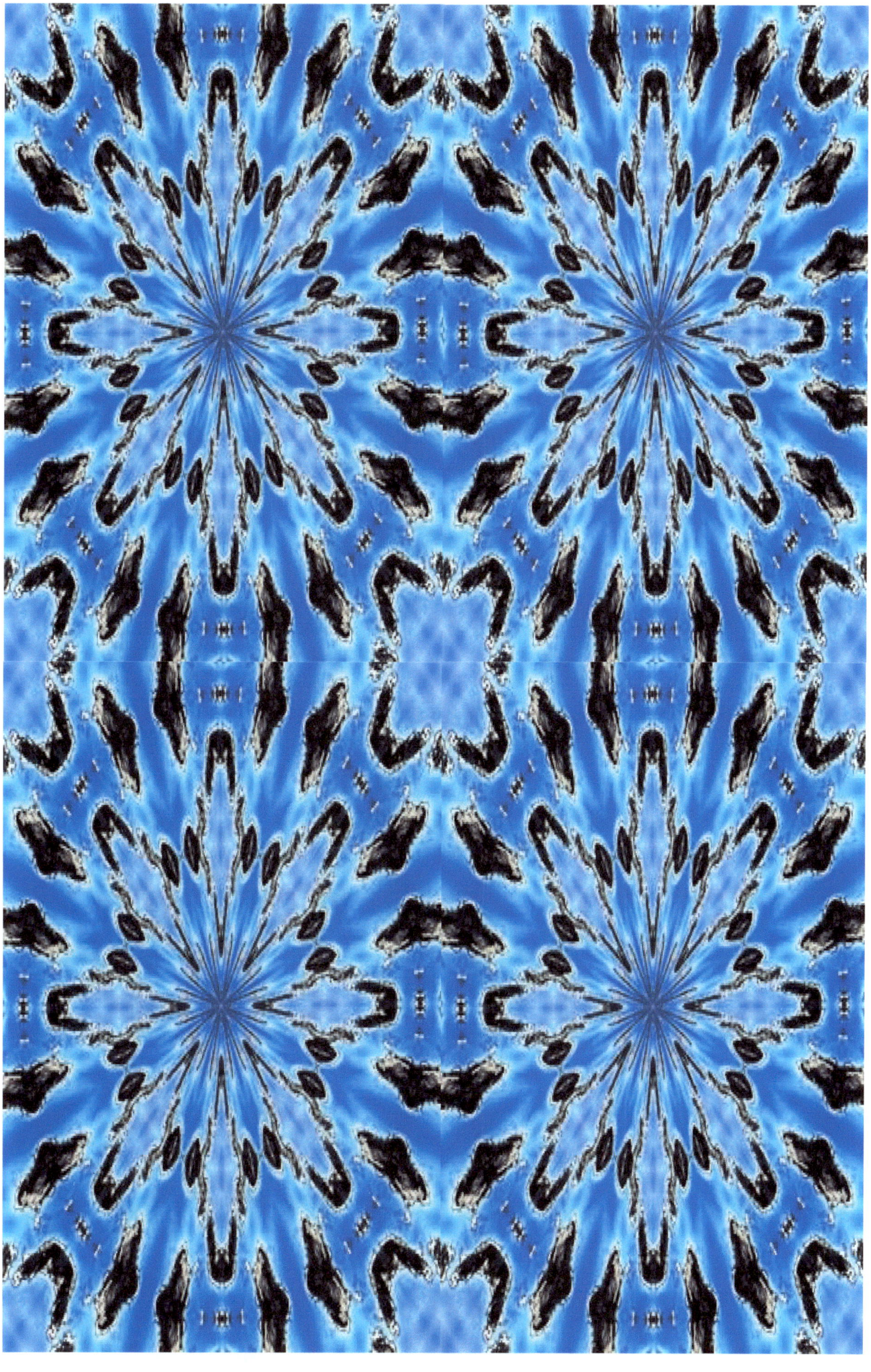

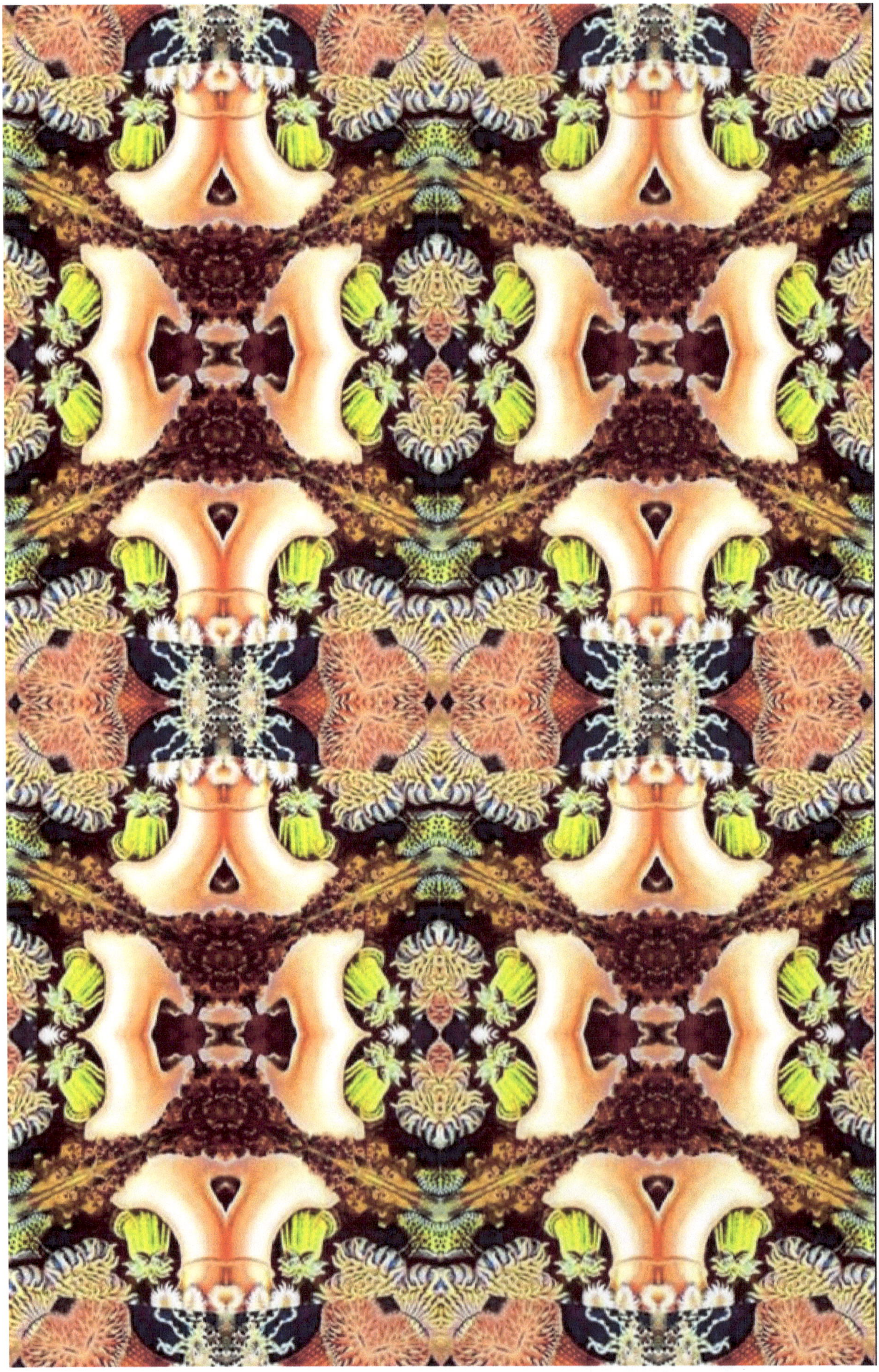

Fantastic Arya Bàhram

www.ingramcontent.com/pod-product-compliance
Lightning Source LLC
Chambersburg PA
CBHW051205220526
45473CB00003B/906
9781718605657